From Our Land to Our Land

ALSO BY LUIS J. RODRIGUEZ

NONFICTION

Always Running

Hearts and Hands

It Calls You Back

FICTION

The Republic of East LA

Music of the Mill

CHILDREN'S BOOKS

América Is Her Name

It Doesn't Have to Be This Way

POETRY

Poems Across the Pavement

The Concrete River

Trochemoche

My Nature Is Hunger

Borrowed Bones

LIMITED EDITION, HANDMADE POETRY ART BOOKS

Seven

Two Women/Dos Mujeres

Making Medicine

AS EDITOR

With the Wind at My Back and Ink in My Blood

Power Lines (with Julie Parson-Nesbitt and Michael Warr)

Honor Comes Hard (with Lucinda Thomas)

Rushing Waters, Rising Dreams (with Denise M. Sandoval)

From Our Land to Our Land

essays, journeys, and imaginings
from a native xicanx writer

LUIS J. RODRIGUEZ

(Mixcoatl Itzlacuiloh)

seven stories press

new york • london • oakland

Seven Stories Press
140 Watts Street
New York, NY 10013
www.sevenstories.com

Library of Congress Cataloging-in-Publication Data

Names: Rodriguez, Luis J., 1954- author.
Title: From our land to our land : essays, journeys, and imaginings
   r / Luis Rodriguez (Mixcoatl Itzlacuiloh).
Other titles: Imaginings and musings of a native Xicanx writer
Identifiers: LCCN 2019035428 | ISBN 9781609809720 (paperback) | ISBN
   9781609809737 (ebk)
Subjects: LCSH: Rodriguez, Luis J., 1954- | Authors, American--Biography. |
   Mexican Americans--Biography. | Racially mixed people--Biography. |
   Racially mixed people--United States--Social conditions. | Cultural
   pluralism--United States. | United States--Ethnic relations. | United
   States--Race relations.
Classification: LCC PS3568.O34879 A6 2020 | DDC 813/.54--dc23
LC record available at https://lccn.loc.gov/2019035428

Design by Jon Gilbert

Printed in the USA

9 8 7 6 5 4 3 2 1

Dedicated to friends and family
who recently passed:

Dave Arian
Alfred "Fre" Ballesteros
Valentin "Cochino Daddy" Barcenas
Trevor Campbell
Glenn Capers
Michael Castro
Wanda Coleman
Ron M. Daniels
Joseph Fabian
Arnulfo T. Garcia
Tom Hayden
Tony Hernandez
Ronnie Kaplan
Greg Kimura
Wopashitwe Mondo Eyen We Langa
James Lilly
Tony Little Hawk
Rene Montez
Isaiah Negrete
Mary Nelson
Nelson Peery
Gamaliel Ramirez
Thelma Hernandez Rodriguez
Jonathan Sanchez
John Singleton
John Chee Smith
John Trudell
Carlos P. Zaragoza
and
my dear brothers Alberto and José René

Overheard at an airport bookstore as two
customers spot a copy of Luis J. Rodriguez's
short-story collection The Republic of East LA:

"You teach Mexicans a little English and now
they think they can write books."

Contents

A Note on Terminology

I use "Xicanx" (*chi*-kahn-*ex*) to describe Mexicans born or raised in the United States. I also use "Chicanos" (*chi*-kah-*nohs*). Both mean the same thing. Xicanx is the most recent incarnation of a word that describes people who are neither totally Mexican nor totally what is conceived as American. It also removes the gender-specific "o" and "a" used in Spanish; Xicanx are all genders and gender non-conforming. This may not work for everyone, but it's about inclusivity. And even though most US Mexicans may not use this term, there is, nonetheless, in the Xicanx areas of the country, a third culture with its own dialect, food, music, and ethnic stamp. This circumstance is similar to that of Cajuns, who originate from the French-speaking Acadians from Canada who first migrated south in the mid- to late 1700s and interacted with other whites, blacks, and Native peoples to create their own cultural expressions; they number 1.2 million people in Louisiana and Texas. People of Mexican descent in this country number more than 35 million. I hope this clarifies what I explore more deeply in these essays, which address different topics but are also interwoven with repetitions of ideas and stories—both between the essays and from previous books such as *Always Running*, *It Calls You Back*, and *Hearts and Hands*— and laced with new anecdotes, concepts, and formulations.

Another World Is Possible

As I write this, more than a million Puerto Ricans march, dance, and sing day after day to remove their corrupt and callous governor from office. Puerto Rico has already lost thousands of people to Hurricanes Irma and Maria in 2017—mostly because the US government neglected to provide recovery assistance and supplies. It has already suffered corruption and economic "hurricanes" for decades on top of more than 120 years of US colonial domination.

As I write this, an international outcry has exploded against the forced separation of Central American children from their parents crossing the US border, as well as the deaths of children and others held in captivity in overcrowded concentration camps run by Immigration and Customs Enforcement (ICE). Despite having arrived as asylum seekers, which is legal under US and international law, my brothers and sisters from El Salvador, Guatemala, and Honduras—and parts of Mexico and other countries like Haiti—are being denigrated and criminalized.

In addition, people have recently taken to the streets to address our compromised present and future due to increasingly irreparable climate change. Protestors and organizations have come together to decry homelessness as well as opioids and other drugs that have led to an epidemic of deaths; gunfire that continues to kill innocent students, shoppers, churchgoers, and more; the fact that the United States has 6 percent of the world's population but 25 percent of all prisoners; how readily police are exonerated for the killing of unarmed Blacks; and the wars without end in the Middle East.

Add to this wave of protest the growing awareness of the fact that we now live with the widest gap between the richest and poorest people ever recorded in the United States.

This moment in history is not just the fault of our current government. We've been going this way a long time. Just the same, fuel is now being added to a burning building. The ruling class of this country—via the White House and its Republican cronies—is working to consolidate an unbreakable base for fascism (among a small but entrenched number of Americans) while scattering the opposition and confusing or scaring off everyone else from doing anything. They're working hard to get rid of taxes that pay for social services—including any possible quality healthcare and education for all—as well as remove regulatory restrictions to allow more corporate theft of land, production, and labor. And they are amassing the most tax dollars into the military to increase their control abroad—and into law enforcement, border militarization, and mass incarceration for control at home.

Key leaders of the "alt-right" have openly said they aimed to trigger the "looney left" with all their misrepresentations and insane policies. Instead they've galvanized a worldwide peaceful, organized resistance that's gaining in strength.

Unfortunately, they've also unleashed a deadly reaction—not far below the surface.

A low-level "civil" war is being waged. As of this writing, since the December 14, 2012, mass shooting that killed twenty children and six adults at Sandy Hook Elementary School in Newtown, Connecticut, there have been 2,193 mass shootings in the United States. In one day—August 3, 2019—shooters killed twenty-two people in El Paso, Texas, and nine people in

Dayton, Ohio. The Anti-Defamation League says 73.3 percent of all extremist-related fatalities in the last ten years can be linked to the political right wing, mostly committed by white males. Republicans and others blame mental illness and video games (although millions of mentally ill people and gamers are *not* going around killing people). There's a pattern emerging beyond that: hate—racist, anti-gay, misogynist, or xenophobic—as the driving engine for the escalation of death in our streets.

Like millions of Americans, I'm demanding a new vision, a qualitatively different direction, for this country. One for the shared well-being of everyone. One with beauty, healing, poetry, imagination, and truth.

As a son of Mexican migrants; as a Native American spiritual practitioner; as a former steelworker; as a journalist and essayist; as the author of sixteen books in all genres; as a world traveler and speaker; as someone who helped create a transformative arts center and bookstore; as someone who has turned around the lives of prisoners, gang members, and addicts; as a man determined to have a full emotional, intellectual, and creative life, I'm compelled to speak out, like many others—not just for the short term, but for the long haul.

Moreover, I'm compelled to help us imagine and realize another world . . .

The End of Belonging

"I'm just a human being trying to make it in a world that is rapidly losing its understanding of being human."
—JOHN TRUDELL

A week after the national elections in November of 2016, a muscle-bound, tattooed white man stood outside a large room at San Bernardino Valley College in California, berating the mostly brown-skinned students trying to get inside. He lashed out about how they didn't belong and were criminals and job stealers—you know, the usual corrosive anti-Mexican rants that have soared in number since Donald Trump's 2016 presidential campaign.

The college had invited Xicanx spoken-word artist Matt Sedillo and me to speak and read poems. A few people wanted to chase off the dude. Security had already been called. I said I'd prefer for him to come in and listen. If he still wanted to rant, we'd handle it. Sure enough, he found a seat among the standing-room-only crowd in attendance, about four hundred people.

I told the group that even though I'm of Mexican descent I'm no immigrant. My mother had roots with the Tarahumara people from the state of Chihuahua, Mexico, also known as the Rarámuri. This tribe is associated linguistically, and in

1

other ways, with the Hopi, Shoshone, Paiute, Tohono O'odham, and Pueblo peoples, all the way down to the Mexica of central Mexico, the Pipil of El Salvador, and Nahuatl-speaking tribes in Nicaragua. In fact, they have ties in many ways with tribes throughout the hemisphere. The Rarámuri are also linked to the so-called Mogollon peoples of prehistoric times.

Just before I was born, my mother crossed an international bridge from Ciudad Juárez, Chihuahua, Mexico to El Paso, Texas. The year was 1954. I'm an "anchor baby"—and so what? Migrants from Europe included many pregnant women lining up at Ellis Island, some ready to burst—more than 350 babies were born there in its sixty-year history. Those migrants knew, because of law, that a US-born child helped their petition for residency and, later, citizenship. Demeaning anyone for making the best case they can for themselves is ridiculous.

More notably, the Chihuahuan Desert cuts a large swathe through the US Southwest and northern Mexico. The Rarámuri have resided in the Chihuahua desert for at least eight thousand years of the desert's existence—way before the Spanish, Portuguese, English, or French; before borders; before "legal" documents. El Paso is within the confines of this desert, which intersects two nations and several states. When my mother gave birth to me across the border, we went from *our* land to *our* land.

During our reading and talk, the white dude who had been heckling students on the way in didn't say a word. Slowly, and quietly, he eventually left the room.

I'm writing as a Native person. I'm writing as a poet. I'm writing as a revolutionary working-class organizer and thinker who has traversed life journeys along which incredible experiences, missteps, plights, and victories have marked the way.

My trajectories have been primarily in the United States but also across countries, beyond seas, through many languages. In spirit, I'm borderless. Nonetheless, I acknowledge the fabricated reality of passports, borders, race, and social classes. I've lived in particular areas of this earth, including where my immediate ancestors have long strode, abiding by natural law, but also man-made laws, some of which align with nature, most of which don't.

I also know this: I belong anywhere.

I belong wherever the earth accepts my footsteps, welcoming my blood, my tears, my presence, as it does anyone's regardless of skin color, sexual orientation, gender, or personal and societal traumas. This is Mother Earth, after all. While we may each have our own particular mothers, she's mother to everyone. I'm not talking about the fatherland—the *patria*, where the word "patriot" comes from—or the nationhood that men created to bring together those with shared history, language, economy, and culture for home markets, governance, and identity.

I'm talking about the ecosystem of a blue, green, and cloud-speckled planet that photographs from space have revealed to be singular—without country or state lines, unlike many school maps, without areas designated for certain religions or ethnicities. In some religious views, it's the way God would see us. In fact, this system includes Father Sky—with sunlight, air, and rain. All this reminds us we are one species, related to all life, varied as any species can be, but still home on one planet that no person, group of persons, corporation, or country should own or control, even if rulers have tried to do so across history.

Unfortunately, with all this jockeying for land, ownership, and power, most people sense an end to belonging. Millions have been driven out from land, but also from their stories and ancestral knowledge. Uprooted migrants around the world have struggled to be welcomed, to feel they have a place to rest and rise. As Mexican migrants say, they feel *ni de aquí, ni de allá*—neither from here nor from there.

Today there is a widespread craving to belong.

Most US commentators, particularly in the media but also in government, have no clue what Mexicans are. We're called "Hispanics," "foreigners," "aliens," or "illegals," but few recognize our myriad heritages, in particular those that go back ages on this land. Identity is also not just about having "papers." One's humanity cannot be determined by documents, and even with them far too many people end up as second-class citizens anyway. Papers don't guarantee anything. It's about full and total recognition and dignity as human birthright.

I understand that to be Native American is to be acknowledged as such by an established First Nation. That's important—for established Native nations this is about sovereignty. Xicanx, after five hundred years of historical trauma, are a people remade to increasingly embody colonial identities. While I don't have direct ties to my Native roots, I've reached back to all of them. Still, what makes me indigenous has more to do with calling on the ancestors; protecting land, water, and planet; and practicing ways that connect me to nature and spirit.

I'm Native because I follow Native ways. I study the Mexica/Rarámuri/Diné as much as I can, including language, rituals, and world views. But being Xicanx is as "tribal" as I can get. Even though I use the word "tribe" here and there, it's not what Natives originally called themselves—in their languages, the names for themselves mostly mean "the people" or "human beings." I also don't seek government recognition. Mother Earth's unconditional embrace is the only recognition I need—she recognizes me, and all peoples, every day I walk, breathe, dance. I'm Native in how I think and live, as a truth-bound human being carrying and contributing my medicine through art, writing, speaking, healing, and organizing.

My grandson Ricardo was born and raised in Orlando, Florida. His parents are good Christians who provided a loving home for Ricky when the world around him seemed bleak, including during the years his father, my son Ramiro, spent in prison.

When he was a child, I'd visit him whenever possible. Once I was privileged to speak at his high school while he was a student there. In 2011, he graduated with honors. Now Ricky's a graphic designer, living in North Carolina, having graduated from the University of Central Florida.

In the summer of 2018, closing in on his twenty-sixth birthday later that year, Ricky arrived in Los Angeles to officially receive a Mexica indigenous name, divined from the *tonalamatl*, based on the 260-day *tonalpohualli* calendar. In this system, every thirteen years of one's life come threshold times, when doors open, the psyche can make big changes, and the body is qualitatively developing. Among many indigenous communities, people would get new names every thirteen years—they were "born again" not just once but many times. Our teachers from the Kalpulli Tloque Nahuaque (a Mexica *danza* and teaching group), Huitzi and Meztli, taught us how to recover the energies and characteristics for anyone born on particular days and at particular times using this powerful and extraordinary calendar system.

That same day, my wife, Trini, was given the name Tlazohteotl—a healer, a weaver, one who transforms what has been thrown away into something new and necessary. I also received my third indigenous name, Mixcoatl Itzlacuiloh—the energy of the spiral or vortex, as well as sharpness: "one who scribes with obsidian."

While many names could have been selected, Ricardo received the name of Yei Iztcuintli—"three dog." The number and *nagual* (guardian spirit) both have important meanings and qualities; in this case, the dog represents loyalty, protection, commitment. In a major ceremony, with family and community present, we recognized Ricky on his path along the Red Road with Native dancers, Native songs (including in Nahuatl and Lakota), powerful words, and a meal, honoring his Mexica and Taino roots (from peoples of Mexico and Puerto Rico).

My grandson is why there is a Puerto Rican side to my family. For fifteen years, I lived in mostly Puerto Rican communities of Chicago, where Ricky's mother grew up. I loved the Humboldt Park, West Town, and Logan Square neighborhoods where I made my home, although now there's been heavy displacement due to gentrification.

Boricuas are *mi gente.*

Besides Ricky, Trini and I also have four other grandchildren—one is half German, the others are half Scotch-Irish, half Hungarian, and half Irish. My great-grandchildren, of whom there are four, include one who's Mexican–Scotch-Irish–Puerto Rican–African American. Who can deny me, or my descendants, a place in America? My extended family is complex and vibrant, consisting of all skin colors and ethnicities, and as American as burritos.

Purportedly, I'm a Latino—or Latinx, as is being used nowadays—although I rarely call myself this. I mean, the original Latinos are Italians, right? Yet Italian Americans are not considered Latinos in this country. And so-called Latinx people have Native American, African, European, and Asian origins, and a vast array of mixtures thereof—not just ties to Spain or Portugal, the biggest colonizers of the hemisphere. Latinx people are known as the largest "minority" group in the United States, yet we do not constitute a monolithic ethnicity.

Let me put it this way: Despite the umbrella of "Latino" above our heads, Puerto Ricans are not the same as Dominicans. And most Salvadorans or Brazilians or Colombians don't want to be confused with Mexicans.

"Hispanic" is out of the question for me. This term originates with the Spanish conquistadors. They were Europeans; the brown-red indigenous Mexicans have different origins. The Spanish language, which I love and speak, as I do English, is still an invader's language. My name—Luis Javier Rodriguez—is only 530 years or so old on the continent. I have a deeper name, in my bones, intrinsic to this land, which I may not know in my head but is still part of my cellular makeup.

Just the same, there are many things that tie together Latinx people regardless of what country they may have come from. In the United States we celebrate Latino or Hispanic Heritage Month from September 15 to October 15, largely to coincide with the independence days of Mexico, El Salvador, Honduras, Chile, Guatemala, and other countries. While Columbus Day is still officially recognized, a growing number of municipalities and counties have changed this day to Indigenous Peoples Day. Of course, people originally from "Latin America" celebrate their own existence every day (these holidays and months are meant to elicit a measure of appreciation from non-Latinx people). We are also into the Fourth of July, Christmas, Martin Luther King Jr. Day, Hanukkah, Native American sun dance ceremonies . . . you name it. So-called Latinos are central to the American soul and deeply enmeshed in the social fabric.

Despite this, we remain a rumor in the country, neither strictly black nor white, hardly in the popular culture. A 2017 University of Southern California (USC) study of inequality in film showed only slightly more than 3 percent of speaking characters in the films studied were Latinx, although we are almost 18 percent of the US population.

We are mostly shadows—and shouts in the distance.

The fact is we are black and white and all shades in between. We include all so-called races, most ethnicities, and many of the world's cultures. Latin America is an ever-evolving reality—as are Latinx people in this country.

In February 2018, I attended the one-man Broadway theater show of renowned actor John Leguizamo. Called *Latin History for Morons*, the show offered important historical and social commentary made palatable with comedy, dance, stage presence, and a familial story line. Leguizamo made the point that it's time to celebrate the richness and expansiveness of all Latinx people.

Let's start by recognizing and honoring how we've bled and sweat for this country. Hundreds of people from the Dominican Republic, Colombia, Mexico, Ecuador, Argentina, Brazil, Puerto Rico, and other Latin American countries, many undocumented, died during the 9/11 attacks. In fact, a fifth of those killed were born outside the United States. Puerto Rican poet Martín Espada paid homage to them and others in his 2003 poem "*Alabanza*: In Praise of Local 100." An excerpt:

> *Praise Manhattan from a hundred and seven flights up,*
> *like Atlantis glimpsed through the windows of an ancient*
>   *aquarium.*
> *Praise the great windows where immigrants from the*
>   *kitchen*
> *could squint and almost see their world, hear the chant*
>   *of nations:*
> *Ecuador, México, Republica Dominicana,*
> *Haiti, Yemen, Ghana, Bangladesh.*
> *Alabanza. Praise the kitchen in the morning,*

where the gas burned blue on every stove
and exhaust fans fired their diminutive propellers,
hands cracked eggs with quick thumbs
or sliced open cartons to build an altar of cans.
Alabanza. Praise the busboy's music, the chime-chime
of his dishes and silverware in the tub.

Alabanza. Praise the dish-dog, the dishwasher
who worked that morning because another dishwasher
could not stop coughing, or because he needed overtime
to pile the sacks of rice and beans for a family
floating away on some Caribbean island plagued by
     frogs.
Alabanza. Praise the waitress who heard the radio in the
     kitchen
and sang to herself about a man gone. Alabanza.

Leguizamo, quoting historians like Howard Zinn, pointed out that people with Spanish surnames garnered many Medals of Honor during World War II; around 500,000 Mexicans and 65,000 Puerto Ricans served. They suffered a disproportionate number of deaths and injuries during the Vietnam War. One of the first known US deaths from the 2003 Iraq War was an undocumented young man born in Guatemala.

We should also celebrate our work in the auto plants of Detroit, steel mills of Chicago, cotton fields of Texas, textile centers of Massachusetts, and fruit and vegetable fields of California. We are among the best players in sports—we've been some of the world's greatest in boxing, baseball, football, golf, and tennis, as well as soccer.

Let's celebrate that we've been in the forefront of labor organizing and fought alongside African Americans against slavery and for civil rights. Let's celebrate that we are among the oldest residents of the hemisphere, as indigenous people from places like Mexico, Central America, or Peru, and we are the majority of this country's most recent arrivals.

Let's grant that Latinx people can now be found among scientists, professors, astronauts, doctors, politicians, and judges; among actors, artists, musicians, and writers. Our ancestors were former slaveholders and former slaves, nobles and peons, conquistadors and poets, rulers and rebels. They include practitioners of Santeria going back to African Yoruba spiritual practices. They include dancers of flamenco and *canto hondo*, linked to the Roma people (the misnamed "Gypsies"). They include Muslims from the Umayyad Caliphate, which first ruled Spain, and later other Muslims, for close to eight hundred years. And Latinx people still use words, herbs, dance, and clothing from the civilizations anthropologically named (though these are not necessarily their real names) the Olmec, Toltec, Maya, Aztec, and Inca.

And what about those burritos? Mexican migrants created burritos and dishes like chimichangas in the United States at a time when they only had access to cheap white flour instead of corn with lime and water ground with a mano on a metate from the old country.

The fact is, whatever is considered Latinx heritage *is* US heritage. Without Latinx people, you wouldn't have such "American" phenomena as guitars, gold mining, horses, cows, corn, the concept of zero, and even various forms of jazz, rock and roll, and hip-hop (the "Latin tinge" is evident in all these genres).

Once, in the 1990s, I brought a white professor to a Mexican *quebradita* dance at a club in Chicago. The best dancers require intense skill, flawless timing, and strong bodies since the dance can be remarkably acrobatic. Many of them wore woven "cowboy" hats, embroidered shirts, and carved-and-burned-leather boots. The professor smugly stated, "Oh, these Mexicans, they're mimicking American cowboys."

"Where do you think American cowboys got those traditions from?" I quickly responded. "They learned from Native peoples, who were taught by Spaniards, who first brought the horses and cows, how to be cowboys. The first cowboys were actually Indians. European Americans also took from them rodeos, bull riding, and even strumming guitars while singing around campfires. Who's mimicking who?"

As we contemplate our place in this country and hemisphere, I have to remind the reader that Latinx people have been among the most scapegoated in US history, certainly during financial and political crises. They are among the poorest, least healthy, and most neglected Americans. Spanish-surnamed people have an incarceration rate almost triple that of whites in the United States, and they are easily found among this country's homeless and drug-addicted populations.

Most recently, states have established laws against brown-skinned undocumented migrants, including in 2010 when Arizona outlawed teachings on ethnic history and culture in response to a high school Mexican American studies program (a judge in 2017 declared such bans to be unconstitutional). Today, Salvadorans and other Central Americans (as well as Haitians) once permitted to remain in the US have lost their Temporary Protected Status—with the swipe of a pen, they became "undocumented" again. And there's that travesty on the border, where human beings are treated like animals.

This practice, unfortunately, has a long history: Mexicans have been widely discriminated against and attacked for some 170 years since the US invasion of Mexico that ended in 1848. At that time, the United States obtained 500,000 square miles of terrain at the loss of 13,271 US and 25,000 Mexican lives. Even though the United States also paid $15 million for the land, this was around $30 per square mile. Thereafter, Mexicans and their progeny were more frequently lynched than any group except African Americans—this fate befell upwards of a thousand people, mostly in Texas. Mexicans were also the most subject to segregation after Blacks; they won court cases to help end school segregation, like 1947's *Mendez vs. Westminster*. In the 1930s, during the Great Depression, around a million Mexicans were repatriated to Mexico even though 60 percent were reportedly US citizens. After US Blacks, police have killed disproportionally more Mexicans and their descendants, as well as Puerto Ricans, Central Americans, and Dominicans, than any other demographic.

US Border Patrol officers alone have shot more than fifty people along the US-Mexico border since 2010. On May 23, 2018, a Border Patrol officer near Laredo, Texas, shot and killed an unarmed twenty-year-old Guatemalan Maya woman, Claudia Patricia Gómez González, who couldn't find work in her village and was coming to the United States to seek an education and a better life. Beyond these atrocities, some ten thousand migrants since 1994 have died from heat, drowning, and other calamities crossing the border.

There's no justification for this hatred, no biblical or literary root. The hate comes from US history, at least the shadow of that history: racism and classism. So while all Americans have much to celebrate in Latinx heritage, like most Americans, we Latinx also have a long way to go.

Whatever one thinks of Latinx people, one thing is for sure: we have given much to this country and have much more to give. We are integral to the nation's past, present, and future.

Alabanza.

The much-bandied-about "making place, keeping place," is mostly to help migrant/refugee/displaced communities get anchored, as deep-seated upheavals drive people away from origins, group identity, and land. We have to take into account the global immensity of the destruction tied to climate change and the poisoning of land and water—as well as that of place, culture, and individual authority. This displacement also happens within cities as gentrification deracinates whole neighborhoods.

Even still, all of us, whatever cultures, ethnicities, or belief systems we may have, have common links, not the least of which is that we are all residents of this spectacular and stunning planet, the only one we know of with all the conditions perfect for our existence.

I once mentioned to a Samoan elder during an indigenous elders' gathering in October 2008, on Hilo, Hawai'i, that my mother had just died. He gave his condolences—everyone has only one biological mother. But he assured me that "we always have our mother," Mother Earth. We should remember in our darkest times that we are never orphaned, that we are cherished just as we are, and that to our common mother, we always belong.

The Four Key Connections

"My generation is now the door to memory."
—JOY HARJO

Yaa'teeh—"It is good" in Diné
Kwira Va—"We are one" in Rarámuri
Cualli Tonalli—"Good day" in Nahuatl (although this can also be translated as "good destiny")
In lak'ech, hala k'in—"I am the other you; you are the other me" in Yucatan Mayan

What binds these greetings, in the languages of a few first peoples, is the crucial awareness that we are all related—*Mitákuye Oyás'in*, in Lakota—every person, every animal, every plant, all living things. This is an awareness that has been devalued in our industrial and postindustrial world.

These sentiments stem from the indigenous mind-set that used to be the view of all peoples, from all lands. But with conquests, colonialism, the imposition of outside religions, and exploitative economic relations, much of this outlook is now considered archaic, irrelevant to a modern world, or, worse still, spawned of the Devil. However, I argue that indigenous thought, spirituality, and science (all as one, as they were never meant to be divided), such as the knowledge belonging to the first peoples of the United States, Canada, Mexico, Central America, South America, and the Caribbean, have deep pertinence to our current societal chaos and to shaping a new and just future for all.

I aim to move thoughts and hearts to the possibility of ancestral knowledge as a substantial guide to where we need to go—first, because every continent has native roots, including Europe, and second, because as the world spirals into worse crisis, this ancestral knowledge becomes a much-needed wellspring to source from as we negotiate the morass.

I will identify four key connections whose severance permeates the present time. In modern society, we have become separated from nature, from our own natures, from each other, and from the divine. I contend these disconnections are central to the inhumanity and disintegration currently confronting Native peoples and, I'll venture to say, all peoples.

The first key connection is to nature, to the laws, rhythms, and energies all around us—in microbes, ground, animals, trees, clouds, moon, air, sun, stars, and more. In the past five thousand years of so-called civilization, we've become largely estranged from nature, its abundance and its powers. With large-scale manufacturing, mining, oil extraction, and such we've created a precarious world. We have false scarcity in our economies. Nature, if we pay attention and honor its parameters and possibilities, has the capacity to give back. It's also in nature where one accesses the ancestral powers, the spiritual AC/DC to one's personal potency.

"Technology [in tribal traditions] takes a radically different form than in the West because its intention is not to disturb the natural world," wrote West African Dagara elder Malidoma Somé. "Indigenous people tend to be familiar with the sorts of technology that do not assault nature, do not compete with the natural order, and do not tend to show them as superior with respect to nature."

Invasion, infusion, and infection by European powers was the single most important cause of the separation of Native peoples from what we consider the Great Spirit or Creator Spirit. This includes forced removal from the earth and sky systems that have sustained us for tens of thousands of years.

Indigenous people knew how to live on this earth, to only take what was needed, to replenish what was taken, and to cooperate and care for each other and the land. They had highly developed spiritual values and deep-seated tenets and ideas. They were the first humans to genetically hybridize a plant (maize—or *centeotl*, in Nahuatl—which became the basis of the world's most important grain). In 1519, when the Spanish arrived to the clean and orderly city of Mexico-Tenochtitlan, larger than any city in Europe, they marveled at the colorful temples, marketplaces, menageries, gardens, and canals, as well as *amatl* paper books, astronomical and mathematical prowess, and fascinating new foods. Only when gold was found did they degrade and denigrate the Natives, claiming they cut peoples' hearts out and worshipped false gods—that they were "savages." Besides enacting the rapid destruction of majestic structures, causeways, and housing, and many massacres, the conquistadors burned an estimated sixty thousand texts.

Of course, there were times when Native peoples violated their own precepts, waged war, carried out power struggles—they are human beings after all. But the consensus around the need to align with nature and each other has always been there, led by the feminine, the first energy, and sustained by the masculine, in the proper relationship between the two core energies.

The second connection we must restore is to one's own genius, the unique internal designs and patterns we were born with. This is where "callings" come from, the act of tapping into the great passions of one's life and evolving the character to carry one's destiny to fruition. The Mexica, like other native peoples, understood this as *tonalli*—one's destiny based on the energies present at birth and that play out, even with distortions based on nurture or lack thereof, throughout one's "dreamspell" on earth. The fulfillment of this destiny derives from deep soul work, but also initiations and healthy community support, as well as quality of struggle so we can give "life" to life.

Remember, initiation has at its core an awakening to soul. And soul is not just about reaching back and down. It also has a powerful connection to the future—aligning one's soul with purpose that serves the world.

For many years, I've been addressing the deep separations affecting our youth under the "profits first" capitalist system. In particular I've gone to scores of impoverished schools, youth probation camps, and juvenile lockups, where I facilitated workshops, poetry readings, healing circles, or lectures. I appreciate schools and institutions that enlarge their vision of how to deal with our troubled youth, advocate for greater access to resources, and are staffed by courageous men and women.

I always have a great time with these young people, sparking intense dialogues and learning by listening to them. Yet, I must say, the separations they face are profound, punishing, and in my view destructive to their spirits and to our communities. What traumatized and raging young men, as well as abused and diminished young women, need is more community, more family; and if they don't have a family or have a broken one, they need a healthy sense of it.

Native peoples know that youth also need elders—without elders, where are the sage men and women who can "show them the ropes" from past experiences as well as guide them through new waters and coming fires? Where are the important initiatory practices? The mentors? The latter word is an ancient concept, from Homer's *Odyssey*. When Odysseus's son Telemachus is without his father, lost and lacking internal strength against the predators who've invaded the kingdom during Odysseus's twenty-year absence, it is Telemachus's teacher, Mentor, infused by the feminine energy of Athena, who steps up to guide him on his ocean journey to find his father, which is really a journey to find his own genius and purpose.

What all youth need, especially the most troubled, is more connection, more stories, initiation, engaged teachers, and guides, led by community—not less.

In our so-called adult corrections and juvenile justice systems, I see the opposite going on. Even the psychoactive drugs we prescribe to ADHD children, or mentally ill persons, or the clinically depressed, result in artificial separation from one's own powers and energies to cope and to change. I understand why, with major chemical imbalances, they are necessary, often lifelong. I have family members who have bipolar disorder and live with other mental health issues. Yet far too many times medications are prescribed when other natural and long-range connective strategies would work best. Instead people are simply expediently misdiagnosed and given pills as the end all, be all of care.

Why is this so?

Because this is what we've done to our whole culture—imposed ruptures from the fruits of our labor and creativity, from each other, from the energies in nature and spirit that sustain us, and prescribed a "pill" to make the pain of those ruptures go away. The current opioid crisis, originally stemming from prescription drugs even more powerful than street-class heroin, is symptomatic of these deeper disaffections.

This unraveling of the human-relational has penetrated our policies, laws, and history. It is exacerbated by divisions between races, economic classes, generations, genders, and sexualities—the powerful from the powerless, the spiritual from the material.

I cleaved closer to my Native roots a year after I sobered up, in 1993, after having been on heavy drugs for seven years as a youth and then drinking for twenty years on top of that. I've been through AA, NA, and Rational Recovery. They are all good. I still go to meetings from time to time, mostly to help others; I recently attended an NA meeting during ten days I spent in Spain in 2017. There are a few people I can talk to about my anxieties, usually those who've been through it. But I have to say it was Native American medicine, especially on the rez, that became my most powerful recovery "program."

During the years I lived out my addictions, my soul/psyche was held hostage. I would do anything to stop the pain from the emotional and psychic losses and traumas I'd endured. I didn't stop regardless of guilt or laws or the fact that I was hurting those I most loved. Bottoming out, which is its own special hell, doesn't always do it. You also need an epiphany, some grace to arise in the darkest hour. Finding this epiphany required years of intense and sustained work to remove those lingering chains on my soul. You have to get to the bottom, to the knotted roots. Recovery doesn't resolve addictions. It merely begins a difficult, and at times painful, process of not using or drinking. In time, you get stronger, braver, more capable.

To quit, I had to accept never-ending ache—numbness only meant my demise. Now constant pain is a constant reminder, a holy surrender. Life is pain. Pain is life. When the pain's gone, so am I.

On June 30, 2018, I celebrated twenty-five years of being clean and sober.

To be clear, society has created and enabled most addictions. On the rez, alcohol, drug, and suicide rates are higher than anywhere else. Not far behind are so-called inner cities, migrant camps, trailer parks, and homeless encampments. Mixed in are those affected by broken or unhealthy families, mental health conditions, and rootlessness, as well as cynical social policies to let drugs and drink permeate destitute communities. For Native peoples, you have to add the enforced ripping apart of traditions, tongues, ceremonies, stories, and relationships. After several generations, genetic propensities drive most disorders.

Societies should provide treatment for anyone who wants it—stop criminalizing and debilitating the addict. Unfortunately, our society thrives on addictions. It's an industry; people profit from our pain. For example, liquor stores abound in the poorest neighborhoods, selling high-potency drinks manufactured especially for alcoholics—we called them "short dogs." I can tell you the brands from my day: Night Train Express, Thunderbird, Ripple, MD "Mad Dog" 20/20, and more, many made by big-time wineries like E. & J. Gallo (although they don't publicly say so).

In addition, all the addictive drugs anyone wants can be obtained on most streets, despite our multi-billion-dollar "war on drugs." For decades, heroin tore through the poorest enclaves, with "uppers," "downers," and LSD thrown into the mix. PCP, crack, and crystal meth have all appeared since the 1970s, when President Nixon began his drug war. Now opioids, manufactured initially by major pharmaceutical companies and presently more cheaply in Mexican drug labs, have inundated more abandoned communities, including middle class and poor white areas. In 2016 alone, opioids, including fentanyl, killed 63,600 people; the highest death rates were in states like West Virginia, Ohio, Pennsylvania, and New Hampshire.

What's common in these communities is there are hardly any free health clinics, bookstores, or decent spaces for community members to create, to learn, to stay healthy. It's easier in these areas to buy drugs, alcohol, and guns than to buy a book. I must also add: a good share of the "recovery" industry gets attached to the gaps and empties, and often makes excessive revenues from private and public funds.

Society has to be held accountable. But to stop using or drinking . . . that's a decision only one person, at the hardest time in their life, can make. It's still an individual choice, one day at a time, every day and every time that choice comes up. There's no way around this. At the same time, society and lawmakers should stop making addictions solely an individual problem with only individual solutions. The courage to begin recovery is rarely found alone.

In most of Europe, drug addicts are treated with a measure of dignity. In some countries they are given safe places to use, with clean needles, under supervised care (so they don't have be in the street with dirty needles and at risk from shooting up who-knows-what into their veins). If they're ready, sobriety treatment is through a nearby doorway.

Free, universal, quality health care should be everyone's right, including the right to be free of addictions. People do become sober, even in the most addictive environments. Can you imagine how more powerful this country would be when the individual's need to heal is aligned with a society that is all about healing?

The third connection we need to restore is to have respectful and meaningful relationships with others. Start with the

Golden Rule: treat others as you want to be treated. Most spiritual practices have this idea as a core value. Caring for others in spite of disagreements, as well as different customs, orientations, and languages, we learn to respect each other as part of the greater human family. We learn to give and care instead of take and detach. There are too many predatory relationships, even in families, but also in nations, religions, institutions, and corporations. There is no need for judgments based on who has money, a certain skin color, or the "right" sexuality, belief system, or gender.

Everyone is valuable.

Often we forget why we need spiritual and moral engagement. It's not so you become a better Christian, or a better Buddhist, or a better Muslim. My motivation for following the Red Road is not to be a better "Indian." The aim is to be a better human being: decent, autonomous, interrelated, and whole.

Jesus Christ never said, "Become a better Christian." In scripture, Jesus says, "Love God above all else," "Love your neighbor as yourself," "Blessed are the poor" . . . in other words, Jesus, like most spiritual teachers, provided parables and principles to help anyone bring more beauty, truth, and goodness into the world for everyone.

Of course, doing this *will* end up making you a better Christian, Muslim, Buddhist, or Native spiritual practitioner. This is the essence of all spiritual practices. Every "way" leads to the same place—a compassionate and more connected humanity.

Let me say this another way: How many "good" Christians do we know who go to church every Sunday, spout scripture like there's no tomorrow, follow laws and pay bills, but are cruel, intolerant, and dismissive of others? You can also find people like that among followers of the Torah, the Qur'an, or even Native American traditions. It's good to respect ritual, liturgy, and custom, but remember these are secondary to the aim—an open and honest heart; close, genuine relationships; and healthy social integration.

While Christianity is the predominant religion in the United States, it is also scattered, at odds with itself. The more institutionalized churches have amassed wealth, power, and influence. The powerful Catholic Church has been racked by extensive child abuse, predominantly sexual, going back centuries. Churches are also steeped in politics, man-made disputes between those who see Jesus as a revolutionary, bedraggled man of the people and those who consider him a Republican.

It has been stated many times that people cast God in the image of themselves. An oft-mentioned example is in a Paris, Texas, cemetery where a statue of Jesus Christ has cowboy boots. In order for Christianity to be taken in by Europeans, Jesus became "white"—which he couldn't have been if he existed at the time he is said to have existed, as an Aramaic-speaking Jewish Nazarene of present-day Palestine. Mother Mary arrived in Mexico in 1531 as the brown-skinned, Nahuatl-speaking "Virgen de Guadalupe." The same is true in other religions—the Buddha, originally from India, in Japan looks Japanese.

In June 2018, psychologists at the University of North Carolina at Chapel Hill, announced a study of 511 Christians viewing various faces to determine what they imagined "God" to look like. The upshot: they chose, for the most part, a face that looked an awful lot like themselves (whites tended to make God white; Blacks had God appear more black).

Beyond God's appearance, a similar case can be made about God's supposed disposition. If people are mean and intolerant, so, in general, is their "God." If they are open and kind, "God" tends to be as well.

Some might say there's nothing wrong with this. Secular interests and images always imbue religious ones. This is because for "modern man," material conditions are primary. But for so-called ancient people, the "other world" was primary. It's important to fuse the spiritual and the material into our lives. This connective relationship is paramount—and has nothing to do with Democrat or Republican, right or left. It's about what's right or wrong—a moral center that maintains respectful and meaningful relationships with Creator, nature, each other, and our own being.

I've personally witnessed many a religious institution full of pageantry and splendor and devoid of spirit. And I've been in nonreligious settings with plenty of heart, vulnerability, ritual, and fellowship, where spirit is tangible and flourishing.

However, politics has pushed right-wing, mostly white, Christians to fanatically misrepresent their own texts, over-looking passages that counsel them to be kind to strangers, as they may be angels, and even ignoring many of their own experiences as Irish, German, Eastern European, or Italian migrants. For them, the politics of fear and division is overriding Jesus Christ's own teachings. And, I must point out, many Christian churches in the United States supported slavery, Jim Crow, Black Codes, and even the lynching of Blacks—around 4,500 Blacks killed from 1870 to 1950 that can be counted (many more were killed, but records weren't kept or were destroyed).

I'm not saying all churches or religions are bad. For years I've allied with faith-based organizations and spiritual practitioners in gang peacemaking, recovery work, and addressing poverty. I've been in talks and trainings with the Reverend William Barber, a Christian minister from North Carolina. He heads the movement for Moral Mondays, Repairers of the Breach, and cochairs the Poor People's Campaign with the Reverend Liz Theoharis, building on the powerful movement Martin Luther King Jr. spearheaded before he was killed. For a few years now, I've been on steering committees and coordinating bodies of the PPC, taking part in rallies, gatherings, and actions. This movement calls for the elimination of poverty and ending environmental and social injustice, as well as the war economy. Rev. Barber has noted there are some 2,500 passages in scripture focused on want and human-based suffering, and less than a handful on issues advocated for by right-wing evangelicals.

"There are false prophets who make merchandise out of the people," Barber says of the right wing's hijacking of Christian values, with millions of dollars at their disposal. "These people *are* religious—religiously committed to the dollar. This is heavily funded heresy."

Barber insists that deep societal and economic change to end poverty is a moral imperative for Christians. If I'm going to collaborate with any religion—and I'm interested in all of them—this would be why. Again, the churches are divided, and much to many people's chagrin, it has to be this way as we reach the "end times"—but not the "end of the world"—of former epochs and stages of development and grow into what's new and arising.

Still many Christians, including evangelicals, are decent and respectful and act in line with their values. They won't justify inhumane behavior by misquoting their own scriptures. Christians have also been behind the abolition of slavery, the civil rights movement, and the fights for women's equality and immigrant rights. We simply cannot have revolutionary change in this country without Christians at the heart of it.

The fourth connection we need, then, is with the divine. This includes what some people call God, Allah, Jehovah, the Great Spirit, or Brahman. The names are legion, but these names are not as important as what they represent. What I'm talking about is the universal sacred tapped into when one is most aligned with one's genius and the genius of the world.

You don't even have to believe in God. You can be as scientific and secular as possible and still find the divine in all things, all arts, all relationships, all humanity and earth. It appears in poems, songs, sculptures, painting, and dance. It shows up anytime, anywhere, especially in timeless moments, whenever the temporal opens up to the eternal. I feel this connection when I write, when I'm in ceremony, meditating, or giving back to my community.

I've also felt this way on a foggy mountaintop, or while watching a hummingbird suckle nectar, or when my wife places her hand in mine. Again, this connection may or may not be about church. The depth of healing in oneself and around us is in the distance one travels between the worlds. For many Irish, it's in "the craic"—a crack leading into the other world—after a long day's work; in a darkened pub; surrounded by friends and family; steeped in talk, song, and humor; while holding a hefty mug of Guinness.

When you have disciplined and engaged spiritual and/or artistic practices, when you interact purposefully and joyfully with authentic relations, you know what I'm talking about.

With these four key connections, we can renew and rebuild our families, states, and cultures. These connections run counter to the current global capitalist society that is based on exploitation, oppression, power, and war. We don't have to keep feeling shallow and disheartened, forced to live pointless lives full of delusions and disappointments. Again, ancestral knowledge must not be dismissed as outdated or quaint tradition. This is not about archaeology, a study of the past, or romanticized notions of indigeneity but about living truths and myths that resonate with the present and future. In these dark and uncertain times, it can show us a way.

There is a story, told to me while I was in Mexico's Sierra Tarahumara, about a Rarámuri man who left the canyons to live and work among the "civilized." Priests and others insisted this was what the "gentiles" must do—"gentiles" being a term used against native peoples who were neither Catholic or evangelical, who mostly lived traditionally, speaking their own tongues, being relatively healthy, never beating their partners or children, eating mainly the three "sisters" (corn, squash, and beans), and walking for miles to get around.

Off on his journey the man went, traveling for days on end, till he reached Chihuahua City. He ended up in La Tarahumara, the native ghetto, and tried to find work. All he found was poverty, drunkenness, and prostitutes.

Without work, or working for little or no pay, he was better off stealing. He turned to thieving, brawling, and drinking. He tried romance, moved in with a woman and had babies, but soon the fights between him and his partner became constant and violent. He left her alone with the children and scuttled back to the street.

Soon the man was arrested for pickpocketing and ended up in jail, where prisoners were locked up and left to their own devices. He became a predator, setting up scams to survive, abusing the vulnerable and weak. After his prison time, he ended up homeless, in rags. One night, while inebriated, a group of men attacked and stabbed him. He found himself in a dirty hospital, as other patients moaned in the crowded room and people lay in corridors waiting to be seen. He was later released, but needed a cane to get around.

After being gone for years, one day the man unexpectedly entered the ruins of a small church in his old village. Jesuits had abandoned the church decades before. A new priest tried to get it going again, but there were no pews or pulpit, the roof leaked, and supplicants sat on the floor for prayers. The priest, a mestizo man in a robe, looked askance at this weary and unkept stranger. He frowned and asked the stranger what he was doing there. The man responded he wanted to find God. The priest shook his head and spat, "You'll need to get civilized first."

The stranger beheld him for a moment, thought about this, and then, leaning with two hands on his cane, responded, "You know, Padre, I've been a thief, a liar, a drunk. I beat my wife and my kids, I spent time in jail, and later, without a roof over my head, I got stabbed and almost died . . . I think I've been plenty 'civilized.'"

My oldest son, Ramiro, also became like that Rarámuri man in the story—trying to find his way in the "civilized" world of barrio-ghetto Chicago. At fifteen, he joined a gang. He later got kicked out of school, then dropped out and used and sold drugs. Within two years, he was involved in shootings, and he began his first prison term at seventeen. By twenty, he had three babies with three young women. After serving almost fifteen years for various convictions, including a thirteen-and-a-half-year stretch for three attempted murders, Ramiro was released in the summer of 2010. By then he was thirty-five years old.

At one point in his sentence, with years to go behind bars and numerous dangers surrounding him, Ramiro decided to get sober, remove himself from gang structures, and dedicate himself to his Mexica native teachings. He refused to go into any protective custody yard—he stayed on the main yards of various prisons. He programmed and received certificates and two associate of arts degrees. He even taught other prisoners how to read and write.

But Ramiro nearly didn't make it out. Six months before his release, one of his daughters, then sixteen, was gang-raped. When he found out, Ramiro nearly lost it. He thought about revenge and other ganglike responses. Even though I was also hurting, I knew I had to stay centered and convince him not to consider any foolish acts. Ramiro had to focus on his release so he could help his daughter through the healing she needed.

To pray for my son, I went on a vision quest on the Pine Ridge Reservation, on the land of Ed Young Man Afraid of His Horses, who carries a respected Lakota name from the 1800s that in the original language meant "Young Man So Feared in Battle His Enemies Are Afraid of His Horses." US authorities shortened it.

This *hanbleceya* ("crying for a vision") was one of the hardest and most sacred acts I'd ever undertaken. In spite of my diabetes, which had just been diagnosed and was at a dangerous stage, I was left on the land, in the open, for two days and two nights, what Ed called the traditional way of counting the "four days and nights" of a vision quest ("day" is sunlight time, "night" is moon time, lasting twelve hours each, not twenty-four hours of day and night). I had no food or water, except for sage water each morning to help with the diabetes. Next to a tree, within a circle outlined by sage, I stood, sat cross-legged, danced, sang, prayed, and wept, trying with all my might not to sleep. In my hands I held a *chanupa*, a sacred ceremonial pipe.

Trini also did her own ceremony next to another tree, far from my sight. In another section of the land was my brother-in-law, a Yaqui-Rarámuri brother, Mexica *danzante* (Aztec dancer), Vietnam vet, and water pourer for the San Fernando Sweat Lodge located behind a sober-living home for parolees.

All three of us went through our own individual visioning experiences on "the hill" as rain poured, thunder and lightning filled the sky, and, at other times, the sun beat down on our heads. My Xicanx brother Tekpaltzin, from Chicago, helped set up the sweat lodge with Ed for when we came down. Also present were our young Native sister Katy Regalado, who had just finished her own *hanbleceya*, and her father, both originally from Peru, who stood by at Ed's home on our behalf.

My thoughts and prayers the whole time, with all the thunder and water and darkness, were with Ramiro.

Ramiro stayed on track, although like most formerly incarcerated men or women, he's had a hard time with "reentry," including having doors closed on him around work. After his release, he spent three years on "paper" and finally paroled out in 2013. His daughter, whom I mentioned earlier, went through more changes, had a baby, and fell into crystal meth and other drugs. She finally agreed to embark on a recovery road to help her second child develop as healthy as possible during the pregnancy. After the baby's birth, we weren't sure my granddaughter would stay with the plan. So far, she's remained clean. Ramiro's other daughter also struggled with life and work, with two babies of her own. They are both now relating to Ramiro as best they can.

As for Ramiro's oldest child, my grandson Ricardo, he didn't talk to his dad until his early twenties when Ricky reached out. Father and son finally spent time together during the Christmas holiday of 2016—they had not seen each other in twenty years.

In 2014, Ramiro moved in with Trini, his two younger brothers, and me in the San Fernando Valley. To his credit, Ramiro has found the wherewithal to pull himself out of the abyss. He's now a Mexica *danzante*, a mentor for young people and the formerly incarcerated, and a poet in his own right.

In September 2017, San Quentin State Prison's GRIP Program (Guiding Rage Into Power), founded by Jacques Verduin, invited Ramiro and me to speak to two circles of prisoners, including a Spanish-speaking group run by Lucía De La Fuente Somoza. One was called the 790 Tribe, being some twenty guys who had a total of 790 years behind bars. We didn't think the warden would let Ramiro in with all his felonies, but he was finally approved. I felt so proud being his father there as Ramiro spoke. He now has the courage, experience, and intelligence to speak wisdom and truth to anyone, anywhere.

Ed Young Man Afraid of His Horses, our great teacher and friend, passed on in 2014. I will always remember the spiritual work Ed did for Trini and me, including the tobacco-filled "Holy People" he had us make for our sweat lodge, when we needed this work the most.

Wopila! (In Lakota: "To give thanks")

All this knowledge and experience informs what I've written about and spoken on for over twenty-five years. I'm conscious that my roots have entanglements—and I try to disentangle what I can from the rest, not cut them, although they are thoroughly enmeshed. For most Native leaders, teachers, and activists, this wisdom is one of the most important intellectual wells to draw from as we ignite imaginations to solve the economic, political, and social predicaments we now face.

These ways are called up to get us out of the habit of the environmental violence we've done, as well as violence to people—their cultures, their beings, their innate geniuses. Even modern science is catching up to the dense awareness and erudition of Native peoples that was accumulated before the onset of so-called Western civilization and has continued to grow since. Here I have to acknowledge the indigenous minds from Africa, Asia, Europe, and the rest of the world as well.

We need to get back to the ancestors to go forward.

How then do we make a crucial turn beyond the world that the powerful and rich, the corporations, a substantial military, and largely out-of-touch politicians have imposed on us? I don't mind assigning blame—it's warranted and documented. Somebody has to be held accountable. Blaming everybody means

blaming nobody. However, not determining specific responsibility, with a precision about who or what has led us here, tends
to lead to blaming those who have been largely victimized and
terrorized into acquiescence. We don't need to pretend there is
no social class to point to for what has become of our planet.
There are already enough apologists and enough subterfuge.

I'm also interested in real, lasting, and deep-delving answers.
Leaving this issue at the level of blame is not resolution, it's not
resolve, it's not revolutionary. We need a *mythic imagination*. In
the United States, mythology has been pushed out of the cultural and social arena. In general, our leaders, businesses, and
educational institutions have replaced such imaginings with
material-based outcomes.

Mythology is not just made-up stuff, as the general public
presently understands it; in our culture, myths mean "lies" and
lies can become "facts." Mythology consists of the stories—the
"dreams"—of a community that contain sustenance for mind
and soul, including lessons, directions, and guidance that can
shine a light on where we're at and where we need to go. You
can't take myths literally, as people have done with sacred texts.
They are metaphors and messages for what matters.

There are many myths across cultures. Michael Meade has
often related a Native American story about the world being a
woven blanket. Its variants include an old woman on the mountain embroidering this world every day, with sun, flowers, birds,
clouds, and people. Inevitably, there's a black dog that climbs
up the mountain and begins to unravel the blanket, inducing
the night, the darkness, the shadowy and fearful terrain. Yet
somehow a piece of that blanket remains, from which the old
woman can reweave the world again the next day.

The Diné make blankets with an "exit" or "spirit" line, seemingly a flaw in a flawless weave. In fact, it is a line to the ancestors,
the unseen world, that indicates there is always more, always a

part of the old to save for the new. This is also true for what may have been destroyed, either by nature or man. Nothing is truly gone unless there is no more fabric left, no remaining memory, no exit line, no more to draw from. Natives on this American continent—and I mean from North, Central, and South America—know intimately and drastically such destruction.

Memory becomes a formidable exit line.

Nemachtilli

The Spirit of Learning, the Spirit of Teaching

"The true teacher is the learner."
—ELBERT HUBBARD

Once, in 1999, I spent ten days among the Rarámuri people in the Sierra Tarahumara. I was taken to a cave where Apaches, who had wandered this far south from Arizona in search of food during Geronimo's time more than a hundred years before, had created a school. A roughly hewn maguey ladder led to the mouth of the cave. To the side of us, several holes in the volcanic rock served as rooms. At the highest point of the cave was a larger area, an opening to the sky, mortared with mud and limestone. My Rarámuri guide said this was an Apache classroom.

The Apaches in those days were nomadic hunters and gatherers. The Rarámuri were mostly corn farmers, relatively peaceful compared to the fierce Apaches. My guide said Apaches were known to shoot arrows down from their caves to ward off stragglers who wandered by.

Those caves shattered what preconceptions I may have had about Apaches. Here was a deerskin, bow-and-arrow culture, also excellent with horses and guns. Somehow, though, these people went the extra mile to create classrooms for their children. I had imagined learning among indigenous people to be fluid, organic, composed more of firm but loving guidance, based on nature's elemental laws and dangers as well as gifts— more like sharing knowledge, not instruction.

In my mind, classrooms didn't fit into this scenario.

Yet, here they were, a testament to how learning had to also include lesson planning, a removal from actual experience, and perhaps a lecture or two from the learned women and men of the tribe. Crude drawings of animals and other symbols on the walls got me thinking there were probably more than a few bored students among them, sneaking in graffiti when a teacher's back was turned.

This is something I knew about: I was one of those bored schoolkids in my youth. Didn't I want to learn? Or was I just too troubled to care—or to be bothered with? I had smarts—I picked up English fairly well by fourth grade in my English-only classes (I also watched a lot of TV and read books). My grades were fine in elementary school. But from middle school to high school, I became a "problem." School became "a drag."

I dropped out. I would've stayed out, but throughout the East LA area, teachers, parents, students, and others had been walking out of schools (the largest school walkouts in US history—the "Blowouts"—occurred in East LA during the spring of 1968). A social movement was afoot—for better schools, better housing, decent jobs.

These efforts were part of the civil rights struggles of the 1960s and early 1970s. Self-identified as Chicanos, my neighbors and I faced similar issues and concerns as other oppressed peoples. I returned to school at sixteen because now I had a cause, something to rally around, to help focus my angers and hungers. I headed a Chicano student organization and led three walkouts, took over buildings, brought in Chicano Studies classes, and even ran for student body office. I went back to school not to be lectured at but to make notable changes in the school environment.

Schools have been important for me ever since. I not only obtained my high school diploma, I was accepted into college. Unfortunately, I never finished after my last arrest. Instead I went full steam into industry. Even now, I speak at hundreds of schools all over the country, mostly because my memoir, *Always Running*, became popular among teenagers and their teachers. It's one of the most checked-out books in many libraries and schools . . . and one of the most stolen!

Classrooms are important. But beyond the critical concerns about class size, standardized testing, zero-tolerance disciplinary policies, and lockdowns, I think what's truly missing in all this is what I call *nemachtilli*, the Nahuatl word for the spirit of learning. Nahuatl was the language the Mexica and other Mexican tribes spoke at the time of the Spanish conquest, and close to three million people still speak it today. In 2003, Mexico officially recognized Nahuatl as among 68 official languages, although most experts say there are 287 distinct indigenous idioms and their variants in the country.

While this spirit of learning is innate in every child, and quite active in most classrooms, the more time children spend in uninspired schools, the less this spirit is appreciated or engaged. One of the reasons for this is that its counterpart, the spirit of teaching, has been compromised or forgotten in too many public schools. You can't have the spirit of learning without the spirit of teaching—they're yin and yang, the feminine and masculine energies active in the classroom.

Anthony Lee, our family's spiritual elder, who also helped establish and taught at Diné College in Tsaile, Arizona, is a renowned educator of the Diné integrated teaching systems. He says true teaching is "prayer in motion." He's not talking about conventional prayer here—it's what's bound up in our intentions. What a teacher is really doing is drawing out the sacred within, praying that this child's life will not be so traumatized or neglected that such callings will be missed or forgotten.

I think most teachers really want to engage this way. But I've also talked to countless teachers who've told me, "Our hands are tied." Most mainstream politicians insist they know what's best for kids. The result is that education standards are artificially low. The standard for reading, for example, is generally at a seventh-grade level for most high school students, particularly in urban-core communities. Why? Well, this happens to be the same level that newspapers, radio, TV, smartphones, the Internet, and advertisers aim at—to impart information, to entertain, and to sell products. I know—I worked in the media for many years, and this is the level we were told to write at.

Higher reading levels should accompany critical thinking skills, the full range of history and science content, strong mathematical foundations, and the appreciation and teaching of art, music, theater, dance, and writing. Unfortunately, too many schools aren't places where true education can blossom; where learning is student centered, constant, and exciting; where interests in life and its myriad wonders keeps growing and the love of books and ideas is paramount.

A majority of schools, particularly public schools, have becomes factories to prepare children to be consumers and "productive" citizens, not active and interested readers and socially responsible creators. In those schools, we insist on certain behavior (zero tolerance) before we even start. We stress out six-year-olds with too much homework (information overload). We've cut out or limited sports, music, arts, and play, although these mediums are also ways children learn. We insist on conformity and passive participation (a few students take active part in school-sponsored events, the rest are spectators). We insist on following rote patterns and direct-instruction manuals. Active and positive imagining are discouraged, monitored, or censored.

There was a conservative Christian school whose goal was to circumvent the adolescent period of a person. "A waste of time," the director declared, without understanding that this period of growth is about finding oneself, gaining access to knowledge and internal powers, and becoming awakened to one's particular place in family, community, and society. Too many adults don't want to guide, to be elders and mentors, so they decide to get rid of this crucial time in life instead—absurd.

None of this has anything to do with providing spiritual nourishment to our children. As Michael Meade says, it has nothing to do with how genuine teaching "combines the imaginal with the concrete, the spiritual with the practical, the artful with the necessary."

As a result, too many good teachers are leaving schools.

My wife, Trini, left teaching elementary school after seven years, and my daughter, Andrea, gave up on the high school level after one stressful year teaching troubled teens (she now works with preschool kids and autistic children). The problem wasn't the students—both Trini and Andrea love working with children. It was the pressure from the administrators, who in turn are pressured by politicians to achieve pedagogically questionable results in the most expedient and, therefore, the least substantial way possible. It was the pressure for teachers to stop being creative themselves, to stop interacting emotionally and meaningfully in the lives of their students, to follow the direct instruction–type systems where a teacher is told what to teach, when, and how, regardless of the particular needs of the children and youth in the classroom. *Don't think, don't interact, don't react. If you show your humanity, you'll be punished. If you show you care, you'll be reprimanded. If you show you're knowledgeable but independent, you'll be ostracized.*

It's time we put a stop to this nonsense. It's time for *nemachtilli*, even in a contrived classroom setting—time to have connected and imaginatively engaged teachers working with children who are already thinking and feeling along those same lines.

To be clear, I'm not against tests. I'm not against guidelines and methodologies and good administrators. I'm saying don't discount or underestimate the human/spiritual element.

What gives us movement, energy, and life is our spirit. I'm not referring to anything religious here; I'm talking about what animates and pulsates beneath our social masks and exterior armor. I'm referring to why people can learn through poetic images over strictly pragmatic directives. This is also about challenging and countering the status quo, to make classrooms organic places for internal and external development.

In this country, we tend to leave the "spirit" concerns for Sundays. But, to me, every day should be a day for spirit (while keeping the separation of church and state). Every day, our interest should be piqued and our challenges incorporated. Every day we should feel, not just think; love, not just withstand; want more, not just do what's expected.

Wanting more schooling? Who does that?

I've always read books. I've always studied, spent time in libraries, kept learning. It's a lifelong thing with me: I love being exposed to new ideas. I'm into science, history, psychology, mythology, philosophy, literature, and more. I have an astounding library—I'm one of those people who can't part with books, no matter how many times I've read them. Yet, I have friends who are college graduates, including from engineering or law schools, who studied late nights and all night, who lived in dorms and attended lectures, who received internships and passed tests . . . Ask them now about reading books. Most say they have no desire to pick up a book ever again.

When my youngest sons, Ruben and Chito, reached the

tenth grade, they expressed how they could hardly wait to get out of school so they wouldn't have to be "learning" anymore. They were both identified as "gifted," read at the college level by middle school, received good grades. But they also insisted on not going along with the program. Even with this confusion, Trini and I inculcated a love of *learning* in them, not of schooling, and they are both voracious readers and writers.

To paraphrase Mark Twain, we should not let schooling get in the way of education.

I'm worried about the "education" of our future generations. A nineteen-year-old former student of Marjory Stoneman Douglas High School in Parkland, Florida, shot and killed seventeen students and teachers in February 2018. Taking the lead from the outspoken student leaders from that school, on March 23, thousands of people marched in some eight hundred rallies in city after city to protest gun violence. In the five years before that incident, there were more than three hundred school shootings in the United States. But the Parkland shooting sparked a more sustained outcry in response to the excessive number of assault weapons in the country. The whole dialogue about schools shifted dramatically to school safety, and rightfully so. The National Rifle Association (NRA), a powerful lobby with many elected officials in its pockets, had never been as challenged, even with fifty-eight dead in a mass shooting in Las Vegas just four months before.

How can you have better schools when parents wonder if their children will make it home?

Still, the issues I'm raising here have weight, especially for the original meaning of the Latin root of "education," *educare*: "to lead out, bring forth." Innovative teachers have extended this to mean to "lead out" one's genius, "bring forth" one's gifts.

The way things are now, with schools chained to standardized tests and inadequate mental health, drug abuse, and family resources, a severe "education" crisis is upon us. In more than two thousand years of Western "civilization," in the most militarized and resource-rich country in the world, this is where we've come to?

The truth is clear: learning is not just about books. A safe and innovative environment for teaching, as well as support for mental, spiritual, and physical health, must involve the whole community—and communities that are whole. Everyone must be in agreement from the bottom up—parents, students, teachers, administrators, police officers, businesses, higher-education institutions, and governmental bodies.

We're far from that.

For years, I've organized and participated in study circles with students and teachers outside of school time. One such circle met once a month for a year in East Los Angeles. Usually, ten to twenty young people showed up, mostly from James A. Garfield High School (one of LA's most notorious high schools). A few kids said they liked being at the circle because they had nothing else to do. Once a young man arrived at 4:30 p.m. and waited, although we didn't start until 7:00 p.m. Another time, eighteen of us went to see the Michael Moore documentary *Fahrenheit 9/11*. Afterward, we talked at the home of one of the students, with her parents sitting in, until past midnight.

In addition, I and others have held healing, talking, and "warrior" circles in schools for decades—rooms where a safe space is established to allow any and all issues, even tears and rages, to be held in council and then perhaps addressed in actual practice and policy.

The point is that learning should go on all the time, everywhere, including (or especially) when there's trouble. There's medicine in such trouble, if properly sought out and utilized. We must learn to stay steady during the turmoil; find our language, our strategies, our directions; and make sure all voices are taken into account.

I assume those Apaches in the Chihuahua caves had their own problems getting children to sit still and pay attention. But I'm convinced it was never as bad as it is now. From ADHD to the growing number of children on the autism spectrum being recognized in our schools to dire mental imbalances among our youth, something phenomenal is happening. It's not that these children are "sick" but that they are symptomatic of an already sick, deeply alienated, and only superficially engaging social matrix. I'm convinced these issues are not just about chemical imbalances and genetic propensities; we now have several generations suffering through the same difficulties. These struggles are due to *life* imbalances.

When we have a country run by people who act no better than street gangs, where violence and force are held paramount over dialogue and relationships, when we have so-called leaders who rarely read, study, or think, then we can see why this is a top-down problem. Children and youth learn from the examples around them—their own parents, teachers, politicians, bureaucrats, businesses, and cultural models.

Nothing short of a revolution in education is needed: a sweeping and visionary process that should bring teachers, parents, administrators, and students together in this time of new technologies and methodologies. We need to foster truly rich and vigorous encounters, where we draw from curiosity, invention, intensity, and risk.

Classroom as life, life as classroom.

This is not about avoiding trouble. It's about getting into the *right* kind of trouble. Whatever we do has trouble in it. It's better to be in the trouble of engaging everyone on a soul level, of incorporating all voices and experiences, of aligning every aspect of our broken communities, of discovering the assets in all people and circumstances instead of working off the "deficits." This is better than the trouble that comes from disengaging, from blaming parents for all that's bad with the kids—or blaming schools for that matter—from just pushing "trouble" out and closing doors to inventive ways to make schools enact the human-making, community-saving dynamic they can foster.

This is not simply about charter schools or public schools—although I'm for the public financing and maintenance of schools, instead of schools that serve private interests.

It's about *nemachtilli*—the energies, powers, and spirits intrinsic to all learning and all teaching. It's about *loving* to teach and *loving* to learn.

Wow, what a concept!

Constant State of Pregnancy

*"And the day came when the risk to remain tight in the bud
was more painful than the risk it took to blossom."*

—ANAÏS NIN

The late Chicano poet Abelardo "Lalo" Delgado once wrote
that being a Chicano writer was like being in a constant state of
pregnancy—always full, heavy with story, in the throes of cre-
ation, but never birthing a "baby."

That's exactly how I felt the day I decided that writing was
what I wanted to do. At the time I worked as a millwright, main-
taining the engines of an overhead crane above four electric
furnaces at a Bethlehem Steel mill. I had on a scuffed hard hat,
greasy uniform, tool belt, and steel-toed shoes. It was a substantial job. I should've been content. Instead, I felt as if my poems
and stories were being drained out of me with every pouring of
melted steel, every searing blast, every pounding forge. Sorrow
came in waves. Perhaps depression is a better word. It struck
me that if I didn't do something about this writing thing soon,
I never would.

The year was 1978. I was twenty-four. To stay out of the
trouble I was frequently in during my youth, I had turned to
industry and construction. I learned skills like pipefitting, rig-
ging, mechanics, welding, and framing homes and warehouses.

This was the right thing. But, newly separated from my wife and two babies, I was alone, afraid, unsure, drinking too much. I felt this was my last chance at bringing out what ached inside, before it became a rotting, dead thing I'd carry around.

I had been writing for years already—in my teens, in juvenile hall, in jails, on homeless nights, or in my garage room. And a few adults in schools and in the community had stepped up to help. Unfortunately, I was unprepared for the possibilities that lay behind my scribbling. I often sabotaged opportunities.

But, finally, on that day in the steel mill, I made a life-changing decision—to quit everything and become a writer, even though I had no idea what I had to do to achieve this. It was extremely difficult to let go of a hard-to-get, good-paying job in the skilled trades. That was all the work I knew, beyond street crime, which I had promised myself I'd never do again for the sake of my son and daughter. While these jobs stabilized and helped structure my life after the destructiveness of my youth, it wasn't enough to keep me—or my marriage—going. I felt a pang in my craw, an inexplicable and perhaps nonsensical invitation from the universe to gather my faculties and write.

My own family and most of my friends thought I was nuts. *A writer? Who writes? What kind of life is that? You should be happy just getting a regular paycheck.* So quitting became an act of desperation, of lunacy, one that flooded me with nagging doubts. Yet it was also a way to avoid dissociating due to trauma and betrayal. I needed to "get back into my body."—to go through a door that opened when I dropped into pain, to not allow anger, blame, and defensiveness to close that door.

The first thing I did was take night classes at East Los Angeles College: creative writing, journalism, and speech. During the day, to bring in money, I worked as a framing carpenter and later as a mechanic/welder. By 1980, I gambled all this away and walked into the Boyle Heights offices of Eastern Group Publications, on Soto Street near Brooklyn Avenue (now Cesar Chavez Avenue). They published seven weekly East LA newspapers, including the *Eastside Sun* and the *Mexican-American Sun*. Run by Dolores and Jonathan Sanchez, Eastern Group took a huge risk, allowing me to write news and a boxing column and take photos. (The newspaper chain finally shut down in early 2018.)

That summer, the African American journalists and publishers Robert Maynard and his wife Nancy Hicks accepted me for their eleven-week Summer Program for Minority Journalists at the University of California, Berkeley. SPMJ also got me my first daily newspaper job, at the *San Bernardino Sun*—when the city had the second highest homicide rate in the country. I saw far too many dead bodies from murders, suicides, drug overdoses, car accidents, and natural disasters.

Unfortunately, due to my activism, a right-wing newspaper editor blacklisted me so I couldn't work in Southern California daily newspapers. I ended up working for a public employees' union during the largest union-representation battle in US history, to represent mostly clerical and blue-collar workers in the University of California system. (The union won.)

To keep my hand in reporting, I freelanced articles on indigenous and campesino uprisings in Mexico, including takeovers of land and government buildings. And I was in Nicaragua and Honduras during the Contra War—at one point, Contra rebels shot at me with high-powered rifles, and they twice deployed US ordnance bombs in my direction. Somehow, I emerged unscathed.

I also managed to write poetry and short stories. I took part in the Los Angeles Latino Writers Association, in its Barrio Writers Workshops and reading series, and in putting out the magazine, *ChismeArte*. I did radio reporting and editing at KPFK-FM (Pacifica Radio) and California Public Radio. I wrote for publications like *Catholic Agitator*, *Q-vo* magazine, and *Santa Barbara News and Review*.

In those early years, *L.A. Weekly* bought a few of my pieces, including one entitled "Raids in Huntington Park: The Question of Rights for Illegal Aliens" (their title), which helped stop the INS policy at the time of raiding elementary schools that left schoolchildren stranded when *migra* officers rounded up their parents. Published in March 1980, this article received the 1981 Twin Counties Press Club Award for Best Freelance Story.

I had a few setbacks: After my first marriage ended, I went to live with my parents for a few days. That's when I found out the plywood murals I had painted as a teen, and had stashed in the garage, had been thrown away. I also learned my early writings, which I had carefully stacked in a grocery bag, were also trashed. My mother thought these pursuits were a waste of time. And another time, I walked into a writer's workshop with a scrapbook of poems and stories. After looking at some of my half-assed work, the facilitator turned to me and said something like, "Man, you can't write for beans!" He was right. However, none of this stopped me.

In 1985, I ended up in Chicago, where I wrote for political and community publications (*People's Tribune*, *Letter eX*, the *Chicago Reporter*, etc.). The stories I covered included police terror, labor strikes, and the undocumented, including how the US government in the 1980s used migrant children as hostages by holding them in unmarked motels so their undocumented parents would come get them—and then get deported. Our efforts helped stopped this practice.

For a while I was in the printing industry as a typesetter, including for Chicago's archdiocese. And I managed a reporter/writer job at WMAQ-AM news radio on the night shift and weekends (in those years, the station was variously owned by Westinghouse, CNN, and NBC).

By 1988, I became active in Chicago's vibrant poetry scene, home of Slam Poetry. I helped create a not-for-profit literary arts organization called the Guild Literary Complex with various activists, including my friend, the poet and visionary behind the Complex, Michael Warr. I did poetry workshops in homeless shelters as well as juvenile lockups and prisons. And I participated in the first Slam Poetry Tour of Europe with six US poets (Paul Beatty, Neeli Cherkovski, Alan Kaufman, Dominique Lowell, and the incomparable Patricia Smith).

After a number of rejections from book publishers, I decided to publish my first book myself. *Poems Across the Pavement* came out in 1989, with the help of book designer Jane Brunette, who is of Menominee-French-German descent. The late Gamaliel Ramirez, a Puerto Rican artist, did the cover art. The City of Chicago and the Illinois Arts Council provided funds. I typeset the book after hours at the publishing house Jane and I worked at. I was thirty-five. This book is how Tia Chucha Press began. Jane has been designing our books ever since.

Curbstone Press of Connecticut came out with my next poetry book, *The Concrete River*, as well as the 1993 hardcover edition of *Always Running*. Curbstone's cofounders, Judith Doyle and Alexander "Sandy" Taylor, worked hard for my eventual impact on US letters. Sandy became a friend and mentor before his untimely death in 2007.

Always Running sparked surprising acclaim. I appeared on *The Oprah Winfrey Show*, *Good Morning America*, National Public Radio (including *Fresh Air*), *This American Life*, and in various other TV, radio, and print venues (including *Entertainment Weekly*). I quit all my jobs and toured thirty cities in three months.

My world changed with this book, which came out a year after the Los Angeles Uprising. It was one of a handful of publications about LA gangs, which politicians and some media blamed for the destruction that followed the acquittal of the police officers involved in the beating of Rodney King.

Since then my writings have appeared in anthologies and

textbooks such as *The Outlaw Bible of American Literature*, *From Totems to Hip-Hop: A Multicultural Anthology of Poetry Across the Americas, 1900–2002*, *Aloud: Voices from the Nuyorican Poets Café*, *Indivisible: Poems for Social Justice*, *Send My Love and a Molotov Cocktail!: Stories of Crime, Love and Rebellion*, *Writing for Life: Paragraphs and Essays*, *In Their Own Voices: A Century of Recorded Poetry*, and others.

Staged productions of my poems, stories, and memoir have been produced at the Nights of the Blue Rider theater festival, Club Lower Links, and the Firehouse Theatre in the Chicago area, as well as by the Cornerstone Theater Company at the Mark Taper Auditorium in LA's Central Library and at the Ivar, Montalbán, and John Anson Ford theaters in Hollywood. A play based on two of my short stories, *Miss East L.A.*, drawn from a film script by John F. Cantú, was produced at Casa 0101's Little Theater in Boyle Heights. In 2019, the first full stage production of *Always Running*, adapted by Hector Rodriguez and myself, made its world debut at Casa 0101's main theater.

I've written poetry, children's literature, fiction, and nonfiction, and audiobooks, e-books, handmade limited-edition art books, CDs, short films, videos, and plays have been created from my stories and poems. More recently I've moved into blogging and podcasts. And I've become a script consultant on three TV shows, including FX's *Snowfall*, cocreated and produced by the late John Singleton, dramatizing how crack first invaded the ghettos and barrios of Los Angeles with CIA complicity.

Tia Chucha Press continues to grow, now with a catalog that includes more than seventy poetry collections, anthologies, chapbooks, and a CD. Our roster of writers includes Patricia Smith, David Hernandez, Dwight Okita, Virgil Suarez, Afaa Michael Weaver, A. Van Jordan, Terrance Hayes, Tony Fitzpatrick, Kyoko Mori, Linda Rodriguez, Patricia Spears Jones, Chiwan Choi, Alison Luterman, Luivette Resto, Peter J. Harris, and Mayda Del Valle. Many of these poets have gone on to win National Book Awards, Pulitzer Prize nominations, Jackson Poetry Prizes, Kingsley Tufts Poetry Awards, and others. Elizabeth Alexander became one of only four poets to read at a US presidential inauguration, for President Obama.

In 2017, Tia Chucha Press released the first literary anthology of Central American writing in the United States, *The Wandering Song*, edited by Leticia Hernández Linares, Rubén Martínez, and Héctor Tobar. Later that year, we published the poetry of abandoned girls from Our Little Roses girls' home in San Pedro Sula, Honduras, entitled *Counting Time Like People Count Stars*, edited by Spencer Reece. Thanks to Spencer, and to Diana Frade, cofounder of Our Little Roses with her husband, Leo, Trini and I spent a month in Honduras in late 2016 teaching poetry to the girls as well as in a coed bilingual school inside a walled compound surrounded by one of San Pedro Sula's poorest neighborhoods.

A recent top-selling TCP book featured the songs and art of Louie Perez, a founder of the renowned East LA band Los Lobos, entitled *Good Morning, Aztlán*.

I'm all about books. Somehow that fading dream in the steel mill found root and soil—even when I received enough rejection slips to wallpaper my house.

The best assurance I was on the right path occurred when my mother visited Tia Chucha's Centro Cultural and bookstore for the first and only time. This was a few years before she died—at the time she was in remission from lymphoma, had suffered through three hip-busting falls, and was in the early stages of Alzheimer's disease. She walked in unsteadily, using an aluminum walker. I began to tell her about what Trini and I were doing with this enchanting space that offered a bookstore, an art gallery, a performance stage, arts workshops, and a full coffee bar. Tia Chucha's, named after my favorite aunt, also drew on indigenous cosmologies from Mexico and US Native peoples, in recognition of my mother's heritage.

As I talked, to my dismay, my mother began to cry. I stopped and in Spanish asked her, "*Amá*, why are you crying? I didn't create this place so you'd be upset."

She then turned to me—keep in mind, I was in my early fifties—and in Spanish said, "I think, *mijo*, you're finally going to be okay."

The biggest hurdle I had as a young writer was learning to write. I didn't get much instruction in the barrio schools I attended, and I also dropped out at fifteen. I do recall key teachers in my elementary school who recognized my potential: Mrs. Graf gave me my first "A" for a couple of sentences I did at age nine, around the time English began to kick in for me. In sixth grade, Ms. Krieger had the notion for me to write a one-page speech and read it to the whole school for Flag Day. I balked at first, super-shy kid that I was. But somehow I mustered the nerve and did it. And then there was Mrs. Isabel Thurber, a school administrator, who years later saw a ream of my badly typed writings and had it retyped on expensive onion paper. There were also high school counselor Paula Crisostomo, a leader of the 1968 East LA school walkouts (or "Blowouts"); Ernestine Bacio, a home-school liaison; and the mentor I've called Chente in my memoirs.

These are the angels that show up, seemingly out of nowhere, at various times when one embarks on that destiny road. These guardians *see* the child, even if that kid is in trouble, mixed up, foolish. They somehow sense a possible life for the youngster, often when their parents don't. Nonetheless, even though I was intelligent and capable, I had to confront the fact I didn't know how to write.

Learning grammar, syntax, and spelling didn't prove as big

an obstacle as finding the time to practice and the will to keep trying even when I frequently failed. I had learned a few things from my working life: to "punch the clock," give it all you got, make mistakes, and keep going, even with more mistakes. I learned what many have understood for generations—the only discipline that matters is self-discipline.

In writing, as in any artistic endeavor, nothing is guaranteed. You may not get published. You may not become known. You may not even be able to earn enough to pay your bills. But if this is the heart of what you care about, then you have to do it and do it as well and as persistently as you can.

Yes, there are obstacles: unsparing critics, friends who don't understand, mothers who get rid of your writing, love interests who don't support your calling, kids who resent your divided attention. Of course, be present to the important people in your life. But none of them should stop you. It's about a primary agreement to live out your inner story—as Michael Meade says, "the story written on your soul the day you were born." It's a story *you* have to bring to life. Secondary agreements are important. These include marriages, children, work, home, status. Don't neglect them. But hang on tight to the first agreement between yourself and the universe. This is the source of real authority, which has roots in "authoring." This is where you enter the realm of ownership, responsibility, and, ultimately, freedom. There are many obstacles arrayed against the poet, writer, musician, and artist in this society. That's on society. But if you give up, that's on you.

Examine. Evoke. Express.

These are the "three Es" of writing as I teach it. Like Socrates said, "An unexamined life is not worth living." Using linguistic tools a writer can dissect the inner workings of one's life, as well as the time, place, and conditions surrounding such a life. "Examine" means that if one is a house, a writer should check out all the rooms, including the basement where the secrets, shames, and terrors reside. "Evoke" means to mine the depths, bring out the grief beneath all the rage. Notice how at the bottom of raging waters are dismissals and deceits—but also excavate the gold beneath the mud. To express requires the use of craft to make music out of misery, give shape to the body of trauma to an effective and captivating degree in songs, poems, stories, scripts, plays, essays.

A resilient and patient person is what happens when heart, mind, and spirit come together, and these in turn intersect with outside energies and relations. Resiliency is having the capacity to remain essentially intact despite uncertainties, fears, and all manner of struggle. It's not just trudging along. This is true for persons as well as institutions. We have to own the problems so we can own the solutions. If we can't even recognize we have fundamental problems, we can't envision which way to go.

What I'm really teaching when I teach writing is not about masterpieces outside of oneself—a great poem, painting, musical piece, or whatever. Yes, these are beneficial. But people who create these works are also in a creative process. *They* are works of art. Ultimately the real masterpiece is you.

To revisit Lalo Delgado's statement, I learned at one point that a baby can only be born when the womb begins to push the fetus out. A baby's first breath sends a signal to the mother's brain that in turn signals the womb to begin the labor process. The baby is actually secreting a substance in the lungs called *surfactant*, needed for the baby to breathe outside the womb. Consider this a metaphor for art, writing, or any destiny decisions:

Be that breath. Start the signal. Begin the laboring process to birth your light.

Poet Laureate? Poet Illiterate? What?

"From start to depart, there's nothing but art."
—SAMUAL N. BROWN

When I received the call in September 2013 from Mayor Eric Garcetti that I'd been chosen as the new Poet Laureate of Los Angeles, I had to keep this information quiet until the official announcement the next month. However, I did mention it to a few people, most of whom looked at me with a smile and a confused expression.

"What's a 'poet laureate'?" more than one person asked.

My so-called best friend wisecracked, "Did you say 'poet illiterate'?"

I knew then I was in trouble.

I was only the city's second poet laureate, following the brief tenure of longtime poet extraordinaire Eloise Klein Healy, who had been appointed in December 2012. Regrettably, her health forced her to step down, leading to my appointment.

Confusion aside, I felt it was about time "poet laureate" became a household term. The United States now has more poet laureates than ever before. There are poet laureates for states, counties, cities, communities, small towns, and Native American reservations (Luci Tapahonso became the first poet laureate of the Diné Nation). Claudia Castro Luna, a Salvadoran American, served as Seattle's poet laureate and later held the same post for Washington state. Two Xicanx poets, Laurie Ann Guerrero and Octavio Quintanilla, did the same for San Antonio. Sponsored by New York City–based Urban Word, there is also a Los Angeles Youth Poet Laureate (I helped pick two of them) and the first ever National Youth Poet Laureate, eighteen-year-old Amanda Gorman.

California's poet laureates have included my colleagues Al Young, Carol Muske-Dukes, Juan Felipe Herrera, and Dana Gioia. San Francisco has also had a mentor of mine, Jack Hirschman, as well as an old friend, Alejandro Murguía, as poet laureates. Award-winning African American poet Robin Coste Lewis took over after my tenure, a great choice for the post. And we can't forget that Juan Felipe Herrera also served from 2015 to 2017 as US Poet Laureate, followed by African American wordsmith Tracy K. Smith, as well as the first Native American to hold this post, Joy Harjo.

The poet laureate tradition is long. Poet laureates were first recognized in Italy during the fourteenth century. Ben Jonson became England's first poet laureate in 1616, although the first "official" poet laureate, John Dryden, received his appointment in 1668. The present title in the United States, however, wasn't authorized until an act of Congress in 1985—prior to that they were known as "Consultants in Poetry."

In ancient Greece, a laurel or crown was given to honor poets and heroes. Such honors were bestowed on the best poets of the time—and those who could best chronicle in verse *their* times. Yet for me the tradition goes farther back to oral storytellers from around the world who've been doing this for thousands of years.

On this land, these traditions harken back to the massive cities and temples of the Mexica, whose so-called rulers were known as *Huey Tlatoani*—Great Speaker—and whose expression for poetry was "flowery songs," which became the basis for "flower and song" festivals (*in xochitl in cuicatl*). One major *Huey Tlatoani*, known to anthropologists as the "Poet-King," was Nezahualcoyotl ("Hungry Coyote") who lived from 1402 to 1472 AD. Knowing this, I once argued with someone at a writers' conference who claimed the "Aztecs" were destroyed because they had no poetry. That false assertion is among the stream of lies offered to justify the terrible destruction of a remarkable people.

The first year after my appointment I was to do a minimum of six events—I ended up doing 110. I did more events the next year, and was additionally given a list of forty libraries from which to choose two to read at. I read at all forty. I also had a blog every month at the LA Public Library's website. I'll venture to say that in two years I spoke directly to more than twenty-five thousand people, and millions more via TV, radio, the Internet, and print media.

I shared poems twice with the LA City Council. I took part in Pacoima, California's Celebrating Words Festival, and the Spanish-language book fair called ¡*LéaLA!* (Read LA). I also read at the annual Watts Towers Jazz Festival, Grand Performances at California Plaza, Grand Park's Downtown Bookfest, and with the California Community Foundation. I read at Beyond Baroque Literary Arts Center in Venice, Sirens Java and Tea in San Pedro, and Get Lit Players' Poetic Convergence at the Skirball Cultural Center (Get Lit also did the first event for me at the Actors' Gang Theater in Culver City and the ending event at the Mark Taper Auditorium). I performed poetry with my friend John Densmore, drummer for the Doors, at the Montalbán Theater in Hollywood, and later with John and Michael Meade for "Aloud!" at the Central Library. And I presented with master African American poet Kamau Daoud at Da Poetry Lounge in the Fairfax district.

I became part of LA's Big Read book events, which during my tenure celebrated the novel *Into the Beautiful North*, by Xicanx writer Luis Alberto Urrea, Ray Bradbury's *Fahrenheit 451*, and the poetry of Emily Dickinson.

In addition, I read a poem in Nahuatl (a language spoken by at least three million indigenous people in Mexico and Central America) for the Endangered Languages gathering at the Hammer Museum with my good friend Bob Holman of New York's Bowery Poetry Club (other languages spotlighted were Hawaiian, Welsh, and Garifuna). I wrote two sonnets and a free-verse poem for the People's State of the Union, a live-streaming presentation from the Bowery Poetry Club. I talked to students whose parents are in prison for POPS the Club (Pain of the Prison System) at Venice High School; did several keynotes for high school graduations, including one of the Augustus Hawkins academies in South LA; read at the Alivio Open Mic in Bell, California; submitted a "Love Poem to L.A." to publications and for a film by John F. Cantú that was shown in area film festivals; spoke at Claremont School of Theology; took part in *Los Angeles Times* Festival of Books events at USC; poetry reading and panel at Mariachi Plaza in Boyle Heights; the Charles Bukowski Festival in San Pedro; and a reading for the late, great poet Wanda Coleman at Leimert Park. I spoke to incarcerated youth at Los Padrinos Juvenile Hall and during the Poetry Circus at Griffith Park.

I also undertook media interviews with *Los Angeles* magazine, the *Los Angeles Times*, the *Los Angeles Daily News*, KCET-TV, Univision, Telemundo, MundoFox, TV Azteca, KPFK-FM, and KPCC-FM, among others.

I helped create the largest anthology of Los Angeles–area poets ever published, *The Coiled Serpent: Poets Arising from the Cultural Quakes and Shifts of Los Angeles*, edited by Neelanjana Banerjee, Daniel A. Olivas, and Ruben J. Rodriguez (published in 2016 by Tia Chucha Press). This beautiful book presented 160 poets from ages eighteen to eighty; gay and straight; black, white, Asian, Native, and Mexican and Central American; Muslim, Christian, and Buddhist; migrants and citizens; women and men. I wanted to make poetry a radical and healing act for everyone, so the city could honor all voices, including those plagued by traumas and lifted by triumphs.

American poet E. E. Cummings once penned these words: "Well, write poetry, for God's sake, it's the only thing that matters."

That statement, by a man known for highly stylized poems, whose own views moved from Unitarian to Republican, may appear odd, contrived, out of touch. I can't say Cummings's words are entirely true. How can poetry be all that matters? Most poets wouldn't say that. Even good teachers can't claim their students are "all that matter." A master mechanic most likely wouldn't say that of cars.

Yet, it's a declaration we need to seriously consider, especially in our culture, where poetry is relegated to the margins, to the status of a "weird" art, a practice rarely compensated or honored outside of a small, and often quarrelsome, group of people. President Trump didn't even consider having an inaugural poet, although Presidents Clinton and Obama both did. (President Reagan and both President Bushes had no inaugural poet either.) In fact, it took around two hundred years after George Washington's inauguration for a poet to read at one (John Kennedy's).

Today, again, we ask the perennial question: Does poetry matter *at all*?

It's hard to figure out poetry's worth when there is a hierarchy of "values" hanging over our heads determined not by nature or skill but by powerful men in the publishing, media, and political industries—entities that are about making money. I'm not talking about family values or cool traits. I'm talking net worth, the bottom line: "If it don't make dollars, it don't make sense."

If that's the case, poetry should perish.

Many of us are among a disparate group of "po" poets. Our main currency is the appreciative applause of the relatively small audiences who hear us. Yet the art of poetry persists in this country; like a genetically evolved organism, it adapts. Poetry is strong among the young and overlooked. It sprouts in movements like free verse, takes root among the imagists, the confessionals, the Beats, the 1960s Black Arts poets (and around the same time, the Puerto Rican, Chicano, Native American, and LGBTQ poets), the formalists, and L=A=N=G=U=A=G=E poets, as well as practitioners of hip-hop, slam poetry, and more.

Poetry in its varied forms of presentation is a staple in MFA programs, thriving in cafes, bookstores, storefronts, schools, libraries, bars. And there are presses—hanging by thin threads, I admit—that only publish poetry and that heroically keep churning out chapbooks, books, and zines. Despite the constraints, poetry continues to be, as British poet Matthew Arnold once stated, "simply the most beautiful, impressive, and widely effective mode of saying things, and hence its importance."

Once, during my first year as LA's poet laureate, I took part with several poets of all colors in reading poems by black writers in response to Black Lives Matter. Similar readings were held around the country to speak out against the disproportionate number of unarmed black people killed by police. Appropriately, the organizer read names of those recently killed, although she also included Latinx people and others.

I read a poem by Henry Dumas, a black fiction writer and poet, who in 1968, at age thirty-three, with two small children at home, was killed by a transit police officer at a Harlem train stop: His "crime": jumping a turnstile (the officer reportedly mistook Dumas for another person). All his books were published posthumously. What a powerful event this was, at the Sweat Spot in Silver Lake, with every emotion evoked, singed by diverse voices, and a catharsis steered by resistance to the continual police murders.

Poetry is not easily monetized and exploited, hence its lack of "importance" in our modern culture. In addition, any upstanding poet would refuse the commercialization of their name and work. Nike once offered several Xicanx and Boricua poets to be photographed by fashion photographer Annie Leibovitz for ads. Martín Espada, Sandra Cisneros, and others, myself included, refused to take part.

Poetry's appeal goes beyond the mundane or profit-oriented. Poetry is a powerful way to movingly and artfully convey ideas and emotions, which in turn is a way to impact and change this world. As long as the world needs changing, we'll need poetry.

Poetry is also how one establishes a shape to one's own life, as opposed to the inauthentic shapes imposed by others, by norms, by societal value systems. Go to the broken parts of life and risk presence not pretense, ritual not performance. Go to the fiery places. Create movable operations that challenge the absences in the world. As in all artistic practices, poetry helps realize our most healthy instincts, including from unconscious ancestral determinants (what depth psychologists call "archetypes").

The "giants" in our world—big wealth, big media, big politics—seem daunting to take on. But poetry can be a David with multiple slingshots, like vivid imagery, clear ideas, and strong narratives in the finest sequence of words.

Looking at it this way, I recall when I was in shadowy spaces, lost, pissed off, tired as hell. Poetry then came and claimed me.

An art, a practice, an inside itch you can't scratch, can do that. When that happens, you may realize the lifelines are inside of you. And this is when poetry means everything.

On historic Central Avenue near East Forty-Fifth Street, the Vernon Branch Library looks like a jail—tall fences surround the circa 1915 building, and a fenced walkway leads up to the doorway. Like the surrounding neighborhood, the library appears beaten down. It's situated on the edge of the high-crime Central Alameda reporting area of LAPD's Newton District. In the six-month period ending November 22, 2013, there were 249 violent crimes there, with an average 145.7 crimes per 10,000 residents.

Yet, once inside its doors, the library is alive with children, parents, teachers, and some of the most engaged librarians you'll ever meet. Inside is an oasis of books, computers, CDs, and DVDs. I conducted a writing workshop there with thirty mostly middle school–aged Mexican, Salvadoran, and African American children. I displayed Tia Chucha Press books and several of my own. I read a poem. I had the children put pencil to paper, including from prompts that opened up their psyches as well as their imaginations. They wrote descriptive and emotion-laden words. This workshop was a highlight of my first year as the city's second poet laureate.

Books. Poetry. Healing.

This City of Angels is indeed a city of poets. And these poets do more than just sing the city fantastic. Many dare to address poverty, police killings, failing schools, mass incarceration, climate change, homelessness. They are bards of beauty and bounty, especially when these are lacking elsewhere.

Poetry is the essential soul talk we rarely find in this society.

Civic society should provide more opportunities to listen to poets. For example, why don't we have poetry at graduations, celebrations, rallies, sports events, or commemorations? Unfortunately, we're in a country that marginalizes poetry, yet elsewhere all over the world poetry is widely written, memorized, and recited, even in the most deprived areas.

In the United States, when a poetry book sells a thousand copies, this is considered a "best" seller for poets. In Japan, poetry books can sell three million copies or more. Throughout Mexico and other Latin American countries, children learn to *declamar*, to recite classic verses from memory. Poets in the Middle East, Russia, Europe, Iran, China, and India are revered; in these countries storytellers and verse purveyors have held audiences entranced for centuries. When Pablo Neruda read at Santiago's soccer stadium, the audience of ninety thousand people would echo back his every word. And Rumi, the Persian poet who lived some 750 years ago, is perhaps the most read poet in the world today.

Poetry, like all art, needs to be at the center of our culture. Our country is deprived for lack of enriched expression, powerful performance, compelling language. In Los Angeles I've seen poetry practiced with strong conviction. I see high school students writing in worn journals outside of class assignments. I see the growing number of spoken word venues throughout the LA area, including every Friday night at Tia Chucha's. This is also true for organizations like Get Lit Players, Say Word, WriteGirl, Urban Word, Street Poets Inc., InsideOUT Writers, Los Angeles Poet Society, Writ Large Press, Red Hen Press, and others, which bring classic and new poems to our schools, playgrounds, juvenile lockups, and community spaces.

Poetry won't solve LA's enormous problems. But with images and visions we can inquire into what can; we can construct bridges across the divides; we can illuminate what's new, healing, and pulsing with vitality.

I finished my two-year tenure as LA's poet laureate at the end of 2016. I waved from a lowered 1962 Impala at neighbors of mostly Mexican and black communities as grand marshal of the Latino Heritage Parade in Pasadena. I served as a panelist at the Southern California Poetry Festival in Long Beach. I read poetry with Shakespearean themes alongside actors, writers, musicians, and others at San Diego's Old Globe theater. I taught and performed at the San Gabriel Mission Playhouse. And I had a public conversation with writer Rubén Martínez at Loyola Marymount University, near Santa Monica.

Even in these times of racial, class, and political discord, there are many healers, teachers, and caretakers we need to heed. They include poets. Please listen. They are truth. They are medicine. They are Los Angeles.

I Still Love H.E.R.

"That's what Hip Hop is . . . sociology and English put to a beat."
—TALIB KWELI

It was in the early 1980s when I first saw hip-hop blow up in LA's ghettos and barrios: breakdancing, aerosol art on walls, lyrical combat, record scratching, and sampled music.

Prior to that, disco had been big in the clubs. I learned how to disco after my breakup with my first wife in 1978. One popular club I enjoyed in Hollywood was where Donna Summer's movie *Thank God It's Friday* had been filmed.

One night I held my sleeping kids in both arms while knocking on the door to the apartment of a woman I had just met on one of those dance floors. Not my finest hour.

On the street something new and exhilarating was emerging, punctuated by upright middle fingers. For context, this was also when the US government, working with Colombian, Nicaraguan, and Mexican drug organizations as well as gun manufacturers, helped crack and guns flood our black and brown neighborhoods. Families and communities, as well as organized efforts to improve them, went into a tumultuous tailspin.

The cultural responses took two forms in LA's barrios. One was identified as Cholo Punk (cholos in many ways were the original punks). This movement involved East Los Angeles youth from areas where jobs were leaving and upward-mobility had stalled, similar to England's working-class rebel youth. Lowriding had temporarily gone underground after forceful street crackdowns. Some of these kids then spiked their hair, pierced their skin, and combined Spanish and English in countercultural rants over grating guitars on makeshift stages in basements, on rooftops, and in backyards. I remember the Vex club, in the early 1980s, where bands like Los Illegals, Felix and the Katz, the Brat, and the Plugz played their minds out; where poet-singers Teresa Covarrubias and Alice Bag kicked ass. The Asco (nausea or disgust) art collective performed art on street corners, and Harry Gamboa Jr. took photos, while Gronk, Willie Herrón, Patssi Valdez, and Diane Gamboa painted enraged images on walls and canvasses. Their impact still reverberates in Xicanx art and music today.

The other cultural response was hip-hop. Okay, *banda* and conjunto music also had footholds, but these didn't really explode till the 1990s, particularly with Chalino Sánchez, Lupillo Rivera, and his sister Jenni Rivera. There were even ska and reggae scenes among Xicanx youth.

But in the early eighties the two phenomena that caught my eye were punk and hip-hop. Somehow I traversed both scenes, knowing how different they were but also how they seemed to be insurgencies against disco. The barrio had its own trends, its own beats, but it also reinvented styles from other cultures, particularly those that related to the poor, the working class, or to Blacks.

I've always had an affinity for street and urban music. Besides the Mexican music my mother played at home, I enjoyed motown and soul hits of the sixties (my favorite song of all time is Marvin Gaye's "What's Going On"). I loved James Brown and most funk, especially George Clinton's Parliament Funkadelic. I got into salsa music, including Fania All Stars, Tito Puente, Celia Cruz, Eddie Palmieri, Willie Colón, and La Sonora Ponceña. In my teens, a mentor introduced me to jazz by taking me to LA's well-known jazz clubs of the time—Shelly's Manne-Hole, Concerts by the Sea, and the Lighthouse Café. And I loved Chicano funk/rock of the seventies: Santana, El Chicano, Malo, Tierra, Los Lobos, and Jose "Chepito" Areas (Xicanesque, though he was *Nicoya*—Nicaraguan).

Having these musical interests is why hip-hop intrigued me. Moreover, hip-hop had five artistic elements (dance, graffiti, DJing, emceeing, and as KRS-One says, knowledge). This covered a lot of ground. I was particularly taken in by the display of language dexterity called rap. Begun in 1970 by Blacks and Puerto Ricans in the tenements and vacant lots of the South Bronx, born of neglect and devastation, hip-hop's first inroad into US popular culture was the Sugarhill Gang's 1979 record "Rapper's Delight." I also loved the multicolored aerosol lettering and figures on walls (having briefly been a graffiti artist and muralist); the skilled, frenetic dancing (including West Coast moves like popping and locking); and the exquisite concoctions conceived on turntables.

In the summer of 1981, I descended into the heart of hip-hop, spending a couple of weeks in the Bronx, staying at the high-rise apartment of a Puerto Rican fellow journalist and his wife. Hip-hop was everywhere—on stoops, alongside gangways, in alleys, bursting out of car radios and sweltering apartment windows, with "writing" on lamp posts, corrugated fences, stores, subway trains, and trucks. New forms of art, technology, and rhythm filled the air. The nation was undergoing a cultural renewal even as it entered a dark American night with Ronald Reagan as president.

Obviously, my ties to hip-hop have been peripheral. But, in one form or another, they were there. As a journalist I interviewed Chuck D and Flavor Flav when Public Enemy were at their height. Slam poetry, which I got intimately involved with in the late eighties, also had ties to hip-hop. I even helped out a few "pirate" radio outlets (low-power, micro radio), particularly among African Americans in Decatur and Springfield, Illinois, as well as Fresno and Los Angeles in California, many entwined with hip-hop. I've shared poetry stages with Jamaican dub poet/ musician/activist Mutabaruka in Toronto and Montreal in 1989, as well as Jean Breeze and Linton Kwesi Johnson in London in 1995. They helped shape hip-hop from Jamaica's own language/ rhythm articulations as well as dancehall, via West Indian migrants in the Bronx and Harlem.

On top of this, I loved the Last Poets in the 1970s and Gil Scott Heron's poetry and music, which many have called the precursors of rap in the United States. I played their albums over and over, trying to master the staccato, blazing tongue-and-mind word fire.

We were, black and brown, in the know before anyone else; hip before it was hip, hop before it was hop. Puerto Ricans and Dominicans were largely into the dance and wall art, but over the years a number of them hit the national rap airwaves (Big Pun, Fat Joe, N.O.R.E., Tego Calderón, and Daddy Yankee), especially with the wicked island sound called reggaeton, and more recently with people like Lin-Manuel Miranda, who created the Broadway hit *Hamilton* (my wife, Trini, talked and read a poem to open for Miranda when he spoke in 2017 at a San Fernando Valley high school).

Living in the so-called inner city, most of us breathed in whatever got conceived among musicians, dancers, artists, and writers with little money or power, preceding mass media and popular culture by years. Of course, hip-hop eventually got invaded by commercial interests with big bucks and became part of movies, TV, commercials, radio, and the Internet. It lost much of its revolutionary content in favor of entertainment, even as right-wing groups tried to discredit hip-hop. Rap albums became labeled, banned, and even burned to control their influence. And graffiti artists, and in some cases dancers, were often criminalized.

Nonetheless, hip-hop spread around the world. Many languages and countries have hip-hop acts. I've heard rap in Maya, Mixteco, Thai, Guaraní, and Catalonian idioms. For poor communities, hip-hop became the voice of resistance. For others, it was an escape valve from the delusional and debilitating capitalist system.

I can't forget the summer of 1995, when I was invited to Rome, Italy, to take part in an international hip-hop gathering, Dionysia Project's "quartieri, the hood, el barrio, ekasi." I asked four members of Chicago's Youth Struggling for Survival (a youth empowerment group I helped start) to join me. They consisted of my daughter, Andrea, along with another female leader, and two Chicago gang members. Another youth, Camilo Cumpian, whom I had asked to tag along decided not to. Soon afterward he got into trouble and ended up doing fourteen years in prison. He later told me he regretted not getting on that plane. Today Camilo is an accomplished artist and one of the city's best tattooists. He recently inked my arm at his shop, adding to the myriad of tattoos I've been acquiring since age twelve, over fifty years ago. This was a way for me to acknowledge his endeavors against the odds.

Sadder still, the gang guys, who were excited and ready, never made it. One, from Humboldt Park, was arrested the day before the plane took off; the other, from Pilsen, was killed in a drive-by shooting the previous weekend. I flew to Rome with just the two young women. The hip-hop heads had heard I was bringing gang members; they were disappointed when they weren't there. One asked, with a smirk, "What's up with those Chicago gang kids?" When I told them what happened, everyone understood. They knew the dangers surrounding gang life.

The Rome gathering went all out to showcase the elements of hip-hop. The city gave us walls to tear into with aerosol cans. Breakdance events were held all over. Turntable and rap concerts filled most of the days and nights. And knowledge spread everywhere. I met pioneers of New York's graffiti styles like Lee Quiñones, Lady Pink, Phase 2, and Futura 2000.

A group of B-boys from South Africa, known as Prophets of Da City, knocked everyone out—they had learned breaking from watching B-boy videos. They also have recordings and videos with music and rap, and have performed for Nelson Mandela and alongside acts such as Public Enemy, the Fugees, Ice-T, and others. Much later, a visitor to Cape Town in the 2000s told me that when he happened to mention my name to a few of the Prophets, they lit up. They remembered me from Rome.

I spoke and performed poetry at the event and even did a writing workshop with adjudicated juvenile offenders. There were about ten of them, escorted by a Spanish priest. They were brought to where I was at, not the other way around. This was interesting: in the United States, juvenile offenders behind bars, even for minor offenses, are hardly ever allowed out until they've finished their sentences. I thought these Italian youth must have committed lesser crimes to be out and about, even with an escort. But in talking to the priest, I found out one teen had murdered a fellow classmate; another young man had planted a bomb for a crime organization, resulting in murder. The priest explained that the Italian juvenile system rewards offenders for good behavior regardless of their crimes. He also said nobody escapes. Even though I didn't speak Italian, I had a fantastic interpreter, and the youth produced powerful work.

Andrea and I also spray painted on walls, me going back to my old cholo lettering. I met Spade, from East Los Angeles, there. He came with another East LA artist who had been shot the week before and walked around on crutches. Spade and I became friends, and he did a wall called *Lost Angels* with an angel figure, cityscapes, and my poem "City of Angels." Spade, who later became part of Homeboy Industries and removed himself from drugs and gangs, is now an internationally respected artist, enjoying gallery exhibits around the US and the world. He goes by his given name, Fabian Debora.

In Rome the rap artists ignited stages with poetic outbursts, accompanied by bold and nuanced beats, in various languages. I got to know one Milan-based rapper named Luca Massironi, who went by "Flycat." He gravitated toward the East LA style, later wearing cholo attire and obtaining original black-and-gray tattoos. He even did CDs with the Psycho Realm, one of the most well-known Xicanx rap groups, and he worked with Xicanx graffiti master Chaz Bojórquez, whom I later befriended. Chaz was known in the 1970s for taking cholo lettering to another level (literally from the streets to the Smithsonian). Chaz arose from the home of one of the most infamous barrio gangs, the Avenues. He's credited with creating Señor Suerte, a skull with a fedora hat and fur collar, used by gang members on walls and on their bodies for protection.

Before I left for Rome, the organizers wanted me to recommend a Chi-Town rapper to invite. The most well known rapper in the city then was Common, a twenty-three-year-old visionary performer. He was breaking out to national audiences with the release of his *Resurrection* CD from the year before. This album included one of his most well-known recordings, "I Used to Love H.E.R.," about the ups and downs, ins and outs, and long, bumpy road that hip-hop had traveled by then (H.E.R. stood for "Hip-hop in its Essence is Real"). His spot in Rome brought Common to the world—and the impact was profound. Common's rhymes and consciousness shook Rome to its core. Just before we all left, Common walked up and thanked me. I've long appreciated that.

Flycat gained a strong following with his fast-paced Italian raps, especially after the Rome gathering. In 1998, he invited me to Milan, where I spoke at hip-hop gatherings in graffiti-laden youth centers and was interviewed on Italy's main TV station. It was the Xicanx world that interested everyone, especially its place in hip-hop. By then Kid Frost, Cypress Hill, A Lighter Shade of Brown, Aztlan Nation, and others had underground status. They combined a West Coast gangsta style with cholo slang and sensibility, and Flycat took this style to heart.

When I traveled to Milan I arrived with a present that caused some grief at customs, but it got through. I brought Flycat a bona fide lowrider bicycle. He loved it, riding it throughout the city. I called Flycat "the Cholo of Milan."

In Milan, I did poetry readings in the Chicago performance style. So Flycat gave *me* a present in return. He recorded a hip-hop–like cut that included a performance of my poem "Civilization." The cut, which also featured Flycat rapping in Italian, showed up on his CD *Una domanda alla risposta* (*A Question to an Answer*), produced and released by U.S.O.P/Skilz to Deal in September of 1998. We also featured it in Tia Chucha's 2004 CD *From Earth to Sky* that presented various Xicanx Rappers, poets, singers, and bands. Here's the poem:

> *There are days when sunshine is toxic, when breathing*
> *   becomes fatal*
> *and the love stares of innocence have fangs. There are*
> *   days*

when caresses are lethal drumming and the low murmur
    of a child's
voice is a hand slap of hell flames across my face;
when all civilization is a squabble in my partner's
gaze and morality is a gun at my head. I didn't make this
    place.
So what if I say you can eat it! Eat it and choke. This
    heart-a-choke,
this diet of hypocrisies, this horse feed of fed horses. This
    salt seasoning
all wounds. Tear it down! Then wake me up when it's
    over.
Should I care if you don't care? Should I sweat the details
    when
the whole enchilada reeks? Just because you wear a hat
    and call
that fashion? Because you love the prison and hate the
    alien?
Don't come to me whining about your lost glories—they
    are the lashes
on slave skin, the gold stolen off the blanket of stones
called our land; they are the tongues cut from wiser
    heads, the deflowered,
dehydrated sirens that called you, then were slaughtered.
Don't cry for me Argentina—or Pennsylvania for that
    matter.
You say I'm no good, but my pathologies are what's
    keeping me
from cutting your throats.
All enslavers. All exploiters. All engravers of God-money.
You who see my children and go insane,
who wear the flesh of Nahuas like shiny suits,
who have Black Hills in your nightmares,

> *who eat with Che's severed hands,*
> *who feed your wives to dogs on cracked plates,*
> *who provide heroin to chiseled daughters,*
> *who bathe in the Trail of Tears,*
> *who sell tickets to the Middle Passage,*
> *whose academies hold literature hostage,*
> *whose culture crumbles in the hand*
> *of a glue-sniffing Chicano child*

For a brief second—ever so brief—I had a hip-hop recording making the rounds.

Language opened up the world to me. I've read poetry at the Sorbonne in Paris; at Harvard and Yale; in Tokyo dance clubs; in festivals, theaters, and bookstores in Buenos Aires, Guadalajara, London, Manchester, Caracas, Mexico City, Ciudad Juárez, Toronto, Montreal, Salzburg, Amsterdam, Groningen, Madrid, and all over Germany, including the Bavarian Alps; in Salvadoran, Guatemalan, Nicaraguan, Honduran, and Puerto Rican barrios as well as many US cities. I read or dialogued with my poetry heroes Amiri Baraka, Allen Ginsberg, Lucille Clifton, and Adrienne Rich before their deaths.

In 2010, I performed in Sarajevo, Bosnia and Herzegovina, for an annual poetry festival established to commemorate peace after the ethnic cleansing wars of the 1990s. People from around the world took part. I recited my work accompanied by an Italian jazz band. The next day, local people stopped me while walking the streets to shake my hand and take photos. In Heidelberg, Germany, I read and did talks for another literary festival and received a painting from a Serbian artist who loved what I had to say. I was also invited to a free meal in the only Mexican restaurant in town, run by an Irish dude! The first time

I read in Tübingen, Germany, was at a large auditorium (I've visited the city twice more since then, including with Trini). I told my hosts that nobody would show up—who in Germany knows Luis J. Rodriguez? To my utter surprise, the place was packed. After my reading, I invited people to hang out with me at a nearby café. I thought maybe five people would show. Much of the audience came, filling up the space and the front sidewalk. People in these countries care, they listen, and they know more about Xicanx writers and poets than most people in the United States.

In 2019, I took part in the first Unamuno Authors Festival—an English-language poetry festival in Madrid, Spain, where I stayed at the Residencia de Estudiantes, a research and cultural center housing university students where in their day Federico García Lorca, Salvador Dali, and Luis Buñuel also resided.

Chicago, as well, has invited me to schools, the "Audy Home" juvenile detention center, universities, colleges, conferences, bookstores, lit fests, neighborhood parks, and block parties, even after I left the city in 2000, having lived there for fifteen years. Famed Puerto Rican hip-hop graffiti artist Dzine once painted an aerosol piece with words from my poems for Chicago's Peace Museum.

A highlight involved my reading at Orchestra Hall in Chicago's downtown, where the Chicago Symphony Orchestra performed, in the late 1990s. As part of the Chicago Humanities Festival, I spoke and read poetry to some five hundred people in attendance, including a busload from the multistory Robert Taylor Homes, a massive South Side housing project that has now been torn down. With me was a hip-hop group from the African American community known as 180. I also invited a San Gabriel Valley Xicanx rap group with strong underground status in LA called D.O.P.E. Mob.

Years later, in 2003, I returned to Chicago to take part in a gigantic hip-hop gathering called Ill-Noize at the Teamsters Hall and Native American Center, sponsored by the rejuvenated Youth Struggling for Survival. Around a thousand young people were in attendance over three days. I read poetry and talked. Among the Mexica (Aztec) dancers, Brazilian drummers, Lakota fancy dancers, African-Brazilian dancers, and capoeira practitioners were B-boys from all over the state, battling.

The other special guest was none other than DJ Kool Herc, known as the founder of hip-hop, a Jamaican American DJing and emceeing pioneer from the early 1970s. Kool Herc (Clive Campbell) is only a year younger than me. So there we were, elders of sorts, speaking to hundreds of youth, many only born in the nineties. I was honored to be on the same stage with one of the giants that started it all.

Hip-hop proved that even with government neglect, with white flight, with big developers burning buildings for insurance and landlords refusing to fix up the remaining homes and apartments, people could still reimagine their "bombed out" South Bronx—what they called "Planet Rock" because of its brick ruins and trash—and create, create, create. This again demonstrates that resistance can have seeds and harvest—that the arts, as in hip-hop, can knock down any barriers of language, culture, economic circumstance, or skin color to speak to the most pushed down and pushed out, and that material poverty doesn't have to mean spiritual poverty.

In 2009, I helped fund the production of an album by one of LA's most conscious Xicanx rappers, Olmeca. His bilingual CD was called *La Contra Cultura/Counter Culture*. Olmeca created a powerful testament to the multitongued, Native-based, revolutionary conscious rap aesthetic. His raps were prayers arising from the natural laws handed down by ancestors, by stones, from our bones. He touched upon deep roots but also pulled from threads of the future to guide us in these modern times. He addressed the profound, the dark, the long-range—the old voices as well as the new. I knew and in some cases worked with similar Xicanx rap artists from 2000 to 2015—like Xela, El Vuh, 5th Battalion, and Aztlan Underground (I once performed a poem with Aztlan Underground in Mexico City's Zócalo during a 2006 books and music festival). Here's what I recorded for Olmeca's CD intro:

Nature—with its laws and manifestations—is our university. The renewal of life, the wane of light, the ebb and flow of seas—all have lessons. The main features of modern culture are deep loss, feeling rootless, caught in the web of temporal time, in survival mode, in the immediate and the shallow. Humanity is completing 5,200 years of an age marked by the rise of so-called civilization—class societies, patriarchy, empire, and conquests. We are now in the precipice of a new age driven by the rising feminine, balance, alignment, and coherency. We are nearing the end of empires and earth destruction. It's a choice more than a given. It requires consciousness more than timing. So let's challenge the status quo, let's create alternatives and imagine the new—underground Hip Hop instead of mainstream Rap; community-based cultural spaces and coffee shops instead of Walmart or Starbucks; community dialogues and youth gatherings instead of mindless entertainment. Awareness not ignorance. Connection not detachment. Integrity not fragmentation. We may choose wrongly. We may miss the turn. We may retreat in the face of the new ground moving beneath us as well as the alignments of the galaxy and stars. It's in our hands which way we go. Ride the change. Ride the movements—Nahui Ollin. *Trust in the ancient teachings. The life force and energy streams of the universe flow through us all. Let the regenerative spirit of* Ometeotl *guide you past the obstacles, diversions, misdirections. Trust. The Creator Spirit has given us all the signs, tools, sacred paths, and clarity to choose. The rest is up to us. Follow the signs. Follow the prophets. Follow the poets. And trust in* la contra cultura.

In 2015, invited by Urban Word's Michael Cirelli, I spoke at a hip-hop gathering called Hip-hop Logic at the Hammer Museum, near the UCLA campus. They were presenting new curricula on hip-hop, which has been taught in major universities and high schools for years. The museum theater's seats filled up fast, and a second space had to be opened up with video to broadcast the proceedings. I noticed I was the only presenter from LA, and the only Xicanx. Almost all other presenters—who included rappers, scholars, and hip-hop practitioners going back decades—were from New York City. It makes sense: the program paid homage to the motherland of hip-hop.

I expounded on Xicanx offerings to hip-hop, an untold story if ever there was one: how West Coast rap, often labeled "gangsta," featured cholo style, such as in the work of NWA, Dr. Dre, and Snoop Dogg (who had a recording and video called "Vato" accompanied by B-Real of Cypress Hill); how hydraulic-powered lowrider cars "danced" in many hip-hop videos beginning in the 1990s; and how anyone with black-and-gray tattoos (this became huge in hip-hop, as well as in professional sports) owes this style to Xicanx youth, going back to the pachuco days of the 1930s.

For quite some time there's been a melding of cultures in hip-hop, mostly with African Americans from the Midwest,

South, and other parts of the country, but also with Xicanx/ Latinx, Asians (the best B-boys in international battles were often Filipinos), Native Americans, and whites. There's even "redneck"/country rap.

All props to the originators—Kook Herc, Afrika Bambaataa, Kurtis Blow, Sugarhill Gang, Grandmaster Flash and the Furious Five, the Russell Brothers, and so many I can't name here. As always, African Americans continue to be the innovators and shapers of the genre; this is true for most urban art, music, dance, and clothing. But it's also important to acknowledge the role played by Puerto Ricans, Dominicans, Ecuadorians, Colombians, Mexicans, and Central Americans in urban arts—not as imitators, as I've heard some people say, but as close and formidable collaborators.

I'm proud to be part of the hip-hop nation.

"Low & Slow" in Tokyo

"Something was going on in Los Angeles."
—SHIN MIYATA

Rows of bald-headed, broad-shouldered young men were positioned in the middle of a small, smoky dance club called Sound Base. They wore "locs" (wrap-around shades), well-pressed Dickies pants, Nike Cortez shoes, extra-long flannel shirts, ironed large shorts past the knees, knee-high white socks. A few wore T-shirts with images of lowrider cars as well as cholas and cholos. In the club's parking lot, adjacent to a lumberyard, several lowered 1950s and 1960s Detroit-built cars displayed airbrushed murals and shiny chrome, the one exception being a caramel-brown 1941 Chevy truck.

It was November 2006. On stage were Quetzal Flores and his longtime companion, Martha Gonzalez, two members of Quetzal, one of East Los Angeles's most popular bands. Flores strummed a *jarana*, a stringed instrument used in the *son jarocho* musical tradition of the Mexican Gulf state of Veracruz. Gonzalez sat astride a *cajon* and thumped a rhythm with her hands and fingers as she sang in Spanish and English, words heavily tinged with Mexican/Chicano cultural and political significance.

They also accompanied a Xicanx poet, reading barrio-bred verses. Even famed harmonica player Tex Nakamura, formerly of the LA-based band War, guest played another *jarana* during Quetzal and Martha's set and with the poet. *Son jarocho*, which combines indigenous, African, and Spanish traditions, by then had become extremely popular in Xicanx communities from Los Angeles to the Bay Area to Chicago. One of rock and roll's standards came from *son jarocho*—"La Bamba," originally sung by Ritchie Valens in 1958 (Los Lobos had a number one hit with the song in 1987).

DJ dGomez (David Gomez) of Monte Carlo 76, another East LA group, stood over the turntables. In between sets, Xicanx street *rolas* from the 1960s to the present emanated from speakers—including El Chicano's "Viva Tirado;" the Village Callers' "Hector;" Slowrider's "Sandoval y Teixeira;" and War's "Cisco Kid." Later that evening, English-language poetry laced with *calo*, the slang of LA's Mexican streets, and Spanish echoed across the densely filled hall.

This could have been in Boyle Heights, Lincoln Heights, El Sereno, or Montebello. It could have been any place in California, for that matter. This music, this style, this way of life, was mostly based in the US Southwest. It's called Xicanx—a clearly defined musical, cultural, and social reality that is also unabashedly antiracist, antiexploitation, and antioppression while also being indigenous led, intellectually grounded, and linked to the social movements that leapt out of the Mexican barrios, migrant camps, and factories in the United States during the last century, particularly at the height of the civil rights struggle.

However, this concert and reading didn't happen in East Los Angeles or East San Jose or East Oakland—it took place in an industrial, mostly isolated, section of Chiba, about two hours' drive outside of Tokyo.

In Japan.

"My purpose is to bring the deep side of Chicano culture to Japanese youth who presently tend to gravitate towards style," said Shin Miyata, founder and owner of Barrio Gold Records/ Music Camp, Inc., based in Tokyo's fashionable Omotesando district.

A short-bearded man in his mid-forties back in 2006, Miyata had invested tens of thousands of dollars, and much time and energy, over the previous twenty years to bring Xicanx music to Japanese audiences. He did this first in 1988 by writing articles in various Japanese publications like *Latina: Musica Para El Futuro* and *Ambos Mundos*, which featured reviews of Latino music. He also penned a column in *Lowrider Japan* magazine that he called "*Que Pasa Aztlán*," showcasing the music, books, and other news out of California's barrios.

Miyata reissued classics from Xicanx musical acts like Malo (of "Suavecito" fame), Tierra, East L.A. Sabor Factory, Slowrider, Mezklah, and the aforementioned Quetzal, among others, some of them going back forty years. At one point, Miyata, out of his own pocket, remastered the music of seminal East LA band the Village Callers, whose original master of their best-known LP from 1968, *The Village Callers Live*, had been lost.

"This was my contribution to Chicano music and culture," Miyata explained. "I pay attention to the mastery, the artwork. I put a lot of commitment into what I do. I do the best work, always . . . I love the artistry. Now with these CDs, Chicano music can find new outlets."

One of Miyata's most important projects was to produce CDs from the extensive Rampart Records archives, known for live shows and the East LA anthology albums called *The West Coast East Side Revue*, first issued in the 1960s and early 1970s. One of these Barrio Gold/Music Camp compilations is *Eastside Soul Classics 1963–1977: Chicano Rare Grooves* with Rampart acts like Cannibal and the Headhunters ("Land of a Thousand Dances"), the Village Callers, Tocayo, Eastside Connection, and Willie G (a singer for Thee Midniters, Malo, Los Lobos, and other groups, he's also featured on Ry Cooder's Chicano-tinged 2005 CD *Chavez Ravine*.

"To me, Rampart Records is essential to know about Chicano music," Miyata said. "I feel Rampart deserves respect. It's very important to the roots of Chicano music."

Miyata set up the promotional tour with Quetzal and company, which included a set at Tower Records in the Shibuya district, two nights at the Bird Café in Shimokitazawa, Setagaya-ku, and interviews on radio and in various print publications. Miyata's aim was to introduce listeners to Xicanx music of the time, and to expand the repertoire beyond what many Japanese aficionados thought was Xicanx music—gangster-related rap.

"Too many times when people in Japan think of 'Chicano,' they usually think of gangsters and hip-hop," Miyata said. "A lot of this comes from US movies like *American Me*, *Colors*, or *Mi Vida Loca*. But this also is because of the push from the mainstream music industry to depict gangsters, guns, and drugs. Many fashion magazines in Japan even feature the word 'Chicano' with gang images."

"I want to emphasize the original meaning of Chicano," Miyata added. While he has also released Xicanx rap CDs, they're usually by more conscious performers such as Aztlan Underground, Kemo, and Aztlan Nation.

"I try to make sure that Chicano music is not just related to gangs," Miyata said. "My purpose is to teach kids the true history of Chicanos and their struggle."

The Barrio Gold/Music Camp, Inc. offices were located in a multifloor complex of small workspaces. Shoes crowded the entrance where visitors, in the Japanese tradition, removed their footwear before entering the carpeted suite. Metal shelving with CDs was one of the first things anyone would notice beyond the sofa and sink in the reception area. In another room were desks with computers and piles of CDs, books, and papers.

A bookshelf surrounded Miyata's desk, filled with titles that included Xicanx classics like the PBS TV series book *Chicano!: The History of the Mexican American Civil Rights Movement*, by Francisco A. Rosales; *Chávez Ravine, 1949: A Los Angeles Story*, by Don Normark; *Barrio Rhythm: Mexican American Music in Los Angeles*, by Steven Loza; the Sandra Cisneros novel *Caramelo*; *The Hummingbird's Daughter*, by Luis Alberto Urrea; and the photo books *Vatos*, with photos by José Galvez, and *East Side Stories: Gang Life in East L.A.*, with photos by Joseph Rodriguez.

On another wall was a special collection of rare vinyl LPs from Xicanx bands and musicians such as El Chicano, Thee Midniters, Tierra, Sapo, Sunny and the Sunliners, and Daniel Valdez that Miyata had amassed at great personal expense.

Miyata probably knew more about Xicanx music than most Xicanx.

I was the poet who read that night at Sound Base, and later at other locations, invited by Miyata to accompany Quetzal, Martha, David, and Tex as they traveled throughout the Tokyo area. The *Los Angeles Times* had a magazine then, called *West*, that included me as a regular contributor (although I hardly contributed anything). Nonetheless, the magazine paid for my trip.

That first night, after fourteen hours on a flight across the Pacific Ocean, and with Sudafed in my system to ease a knock-me-on-my-ass cold, I felt like a zombie. My brain was seemingly filled with cotton. But I performed my poems, like I always did, as if I had my wits about me—the show had to go on.

I stayed in a mirrored hotel room in a largely transgender community, with male, female, and gender nonconforming sex workers on the street—apparently among the cheapest rooms available.

When I wasn't accompanying Miyata and my East LA friends, I walked around the vast city, the world's largest, checking out shops, beautifully kept parks, and interesting neighborhoods. I bought manga magazines for my young sons, who loved anime and other Japanese art forms. I rode the subway system with queer Afro-Peruvian artist Favianna Rodriguez, who was in Japan at the time studying printmaking. She showed me many sights, and we had great talks about art, music, and the Japanese-Xicanx connection.

In the late 1960s, my brother José owned a 1957 Chevy Bel Air that we worked on together—placing it over cinderblocks to put in brakes, or tuning and timing the engine inside an open hood. We learned by following the instructions in car-repair books, or by putting our hands in the grease, so to speak. Once, when I was thirteen, I held up a transmission with a two-by-four board as my brother—three years older than me—lay under the propped-up car wrenching nuts and bolts. At one point, I lost my grip, and the gearbox fell on José's chest. He yelled, and I ran off, knowing how mad he'd get. But he was fine.

José and I have laughed about that incident for years.

Around age sixteen, three homies and I collectively owned a 1963 Chevy Impala—we tinkered with the car together and lowered it the old-fashioned way, by cutting the tire springs. We glided "the tre" on cruise nights down East Los Angeles's Whittier Boulevard, *rolas* blaring from bass-heavy stereo players, cars "dancing" on the road with hydraulic lifts, lowrider hats and shades on dudes with tattooed arms hanging over car doors, and big-haired girls sitting high on convertibles in the most strikingly beautiful dresses, with dark eyes and smiles.

One day, one of the homies crashed the Impala—and that was that.

At eighteen, the first car I ever personally owned was a silver flake–blue lowered 1968 VW Bug with magnesium hubcaps on wheels that protruded inches from the body. I drove this baby till the bumpers fell off.

After my first marriage, I obtained a 1954 Chevy Bel Air. I worked on this car constantly, lowered it, even took off the engine from its mounts, rebored cylinders, and then put it back together. I enjoyed working on that car, even when my first wife accused me of loving it more than her. I sold that car for a lousy $250 after our marriage broke up. I had gotten laid off and needed funds.

How stupid was that?!

I've never had another lowrider since. Monetarily it wasn't feasible, as customizing involved more complex and expensive lifts, chrome or gold-plated metal, and extravagant murals. Not that I didn't appreciate a well-designed and beautifully kept *ranfla*. I continued to show up at lowrider shows. And in the late 1970s, I freelanced as a photographer and writer for *Q-vo*, a lowrider magazine.

I remain a lifelong follower of lowrider culture.

I was amazed at how the Japanese aficionados kept this tradition alive. At the time, Japanese buyers were paying from $30,000 to $50,000 for Xicanx-created cars from LA with hydraulics, magnesium wheels, chain steering wheels, and colorful airbrushed murals. One official at LA's harbor told me Japanese products arrived in large container ships. Mostly lowrider cars shipped out to Japan.

Unfortunately, the Los Angeles County's Sheriff's Department and Los Angeles Police Department had outlawed lowriding on the streets. Most lowrider cars were kept in garages or protected safe spots until the next lowrider show at fairgrounds, parks, or malls. Yet lowriders and LA's murals (and later aerosol graffiti) brought tourist dollars to the area, perhaps more than well-known haunts like Hollywood or Venice Beach.

Despite this, for decades there was no official support for lowriders, murals, or graffiti (which was also outlawed with graffiti abatement ordinances). What Los Angeles street life offered to the world was officially rejected, although recognized and valued worldwide.

From the 1950s to the 1970s, Los Angeles was famous for regional cruising scenes, including Whittier Boulevard, the mother of all cruising spots, and the San Fernando Valley's Van Nuys Boulevard. East LA's seminal band of the 1960s, Thee Midniters, had a regional hit with the 1965 cruising anthem "Whittier Blvd."

Then, in March 1979, law enforcement officials closed off the main cruising sections of Whittier Boulevard. In the ensuing melee, officers arrested some six hundred people, many of whom were beaten. Nationally syndicated columnist Roberto Rodriguez wrote a self-published memoir of this crackdown in 1984 called *Assault with a Deadly Weapon*. He documented the beating he suffered at the hands of sheriff's deputies (the "deadly weapon" in question was his camera). Rodriguez reported that after the beating, deputies arrested him for assault with a deadly weapon and assault and battery on a police officer, although he was only covering the scene for *Lowrider* magazine. He was hospitalized for several days and still suffering headaches at the time he wrote about the attack. Rodriguez later received a $200,000 settlement from the Los Angeles County Sheriff's Department.

Xicanx youth created lowriding with cars that Detroit cast off for newer models in the 1930s, tied to the pachuco culture of the time. By the 1950s, lowriding became a nexus of black and brown urban reality; African Americans, who influenced Mexican Americans in music and style, were in turn influenced by Xicanx street creations. There were a number of African American car clubs, and many African American fans showed up to Xicanx car shows. Later in the 1990s, when West Coast hip-hop turned the hip-hop world upside down, lowrider cars featured prominently in rap music videos.

In fact, the LA band War, the musical group that captured the Xicanx street style of the 1970s, consisted mostly of African Americans. In 1975, War made the theme song of all theme songs for this culture—"Lowrider."

In 2006, I did a poetry reading with the Jump Start Performance Company in San Antonio, Texas, exalting lowrider culture, with the theme of "Suavecito." A local car club, La Familia, had a display of vintage lowered cars and trucks. Lowrider bikes hung from the ceiling. Aerosol spray art covered the back wall. Also reading were Levi Romero of Albuquerque, New Mexico, renowned for his lowrider poems, and the great Xicanx writer Sandra Cisneros.

Then, in 2009, Los Angeles's Department of Cultural Affairs reversed years of neglecting lowriding culture when it obtained a federal grant for several writers and artists to attend that year's Guadalajara Book Festival in Mexico, the largest book festival in the Western Hemisphere. Tia Chucha's Centro Cultural became one of the grant recipients. Besides having me read and take part in panels, as well as display Tia Chucha Press books, we were provided funds to present two lowrider cars, two lowrider bikes, and a short film called "Living La Vida Lowrider."

Denise Sandoval, a Chicano Studies professor at California State University, Northridge, gathered the cars, bikes, and film. Sandoval is a leading expert on lowriding. Over the years, she's written extensively on the culture and curated lowriding and related art exhibits at the Petersen Automotive Museum on LA's west side, including "La Vida Lowrider: Cruising the City of Los Angeles" and "The High Art of Riding Low: Ranflas, Corazón e Inspiracíon."

The lowrider display we brought to the Guadalajara Book Festival became a hit, the first of its kind in Mexico. We had the famous "Mexican Pride" car by Chino Vega, among others. Mexican media interviewed all of us. Even deported Xicanx youth came to tell us they had lowrider cars and bikes, mostly hidden away. One afternoon a number of them brought their vehicles to the parking lot of the book festival, creating an impromptu lowriding show.

Xicanx pride in Mexico.

"I first found out about Chicano culture from the movies and TV," Shin Miyata said. "The TV show *CHiPs*, for example, was for a time very popular in Japan. I liked Ponch [the role played by Erik Estrada]. There was even one *CHiPs* show with Eddie James Olmos in it—he was very young then. I also recall a 1979 movie called Boulevard Nights [starring Richard Yñiguez and Danny De La Paz] with lowrider cars and people speaking Spanish as well as English with an accent. The youth in this movie had a unique fashion: baggy pants, bandanas—I felt it was cool. Gradually, I figured that something was going on in Los Angeles. After I graduated high school, I went to a Japanese university to learn Spanish. But while some students wanted to go to Spain or Latin America to practice the language and study, I was already interested in Chicanos. So, in 1984, I went to LA"

"In LA, I didn't go to Hollywood or Santa Monica like others might do," Miyata continued. "I went directly to East LA, which I found on a map. I walked into a Mexican restaurant on Whittier Boulevard. The restaurant had a jukebox where I found

songs from the band Tierra. I knew I wanted to hear more of
this music. I then brought Chicano music to Japan. The first
Chicano LP I bought was *Tierra*, in 1981 or 1982. I also got music
from Texas, including accordion music known as 'Tejano.'"

After taking off a year from Kanagawa University, near
Tokyo, Miyata decided to spend that time in East LA—he stayed
in City Terrace and Boyle Heights. Miyata had met a reverend
from Japan at an English school on Wilshire Boulevard who
had started work at an old Buddhist temple on First Street. This
reverend introduced Miyata to a Xicanx family to stay with. The
family was part of a church near the Ramona Gardens housing
project. To help make ends meet, he taught judo for a time at
the church.

In May 1985, at age twenty-two, Miyata attended a free Cinco
de Mayo concert in Lincoln Park, in East LA's Lincoln Heights,
to see Los Lobos—the biggest band to come out of East LA—
and another well-known east side band, Califas. There he met
Rodrigo Hernandez, a factory worker who ended up inviting
Miyata to stay with his family. Hernandez introduced Miyata to
the East LA lowrider car scene, including shows at spots like the
Pico Rivera Sports Arena and the Los Angeles Coliseum.

"Rodrigo showed me a lot about Chicano music, history,
and the meaning of it all," Miyata recalled. "We used to cruise
down Whittier Boulevard at midnight, listening to these
sounds, including the old Sancho (Daniel Castro) radio show.
I remember how Rodrigo loved to listen to bands like War and
Malo—that's how I got to know who they were."

When Miyata returned to Japan, he began writing on Chicano music and culture. His articles included interviews with
Tierra singers Steve and Rudy Salas (Tierra, according to their
website, was the first Latino group to have four songs on the
national charts, and two simultaneously in the Top 100); Xicanx
Latin jazz conga player Poncho Sanchez; Xicanx rapper Kid

Frost (now known as Frost); Esteban Jordan, of Tejano music fame; and the late, great Xicanx singer Freddy Fender ("Wasted Days and Wasted Nights," among other hits).

"I wrote around two hundred articles in various magazines," Miyata said. "I even went to San Antonio for a Tejano music festival. I had to pay for the whole trip myself—I spent so much money, but it was worth it."

In 1988, Miyata wrote for *Custom Car* magazine in Japan. He did the first piece on the Los Angeles lowriding scene there. The magazine was so impressed with the work, they gave Miyata his own page every month. In 1991, a spin-off of *Custom Car* was born called *Lowrider Japan*. They in turn obtained license to use the original California-based *Lowrider* magazine logo. At its height, Miyata claims, *Lowrider Japan* reached 150,000 readers; by the time we talked the circulation had dropped closer to 70,000. He also wrote about the first lowrider show in Japan, in 1994. Miyata continued to do a column in the magazine, making him well known in the Japanese lowriding world.

A perusal through the hefty magazine—read from back to front as most books and magazines are in Japan—showed how big this world had become. Many Japanese car shows and car clubs were featured in its pages, including lowrider bike clubs, most of which emulated the names and styles of their LA counterparts: Califelos Car Club, Ride IV Life, *Hermanos* Car Club, Street Life Car Club, and more.

A page called "Lowrider *Arte*" demonstrated Xicanx-style street drawings. Advertisement featured shops specializing in tire rims, hydraulics, and mountains of accessories. There were also ads to buy older US-made car models. And space was reserved for clothing stores featuring cholo and hip-hop attire, including five pages of lowrider-wear shop listings. Most of this, except for the lettering and the Japanese women and men whose images embellished the magazine, appeared as in the original *Lowrider* publication.

The skyline at night spread jaggedly across Tokyo Bay for miles. The lights in Shinjuku or Shibuya, world-renowned walking districts, were penetrating, colorful, dazzling. Multi-story neon signs and video billboards flashed so brightly it felt like daytime.

People were extraordinarily orderly and also extremely polite. The Japanese word I heard often was *arigato*—thank you. This only seemed out of place in my mind because of living in the United States, especially in the poorer working-class areas like the barrios of California or Chicago. In the United States, most things were in your face. People pretty much told you what was on their mind—sometimes they could be kind, often not. I'm not saying one culture was better than the other. They were just different.

For days I walked around, taking in the sounds, the flavors, the people, under the spell of this world-class city. The streets appeared void of street vendors and children, yet it streamed along to a clearly defined urban pulse.

A myriad of sights and smells sprang at me, including tons of advertisements—so many products to sell. This city was the epitome of modern commercialization. Many people I saw wore business suits. There was no escaping the layers of com-modification.

On one holiday, I noticed thousands of people in the street. I thought it was a protest—something I was used to in LA, but also because of having just come from Mexico City, where pro-tests and marches were endless.

When I witnessed the multitudes on the street in Tokyo, I climbed a cement wall for a better view, trying to surmise what issue they were addressing. To my amazement I discovered this throng had not gathered to protest—they had amassed to go shopping. I soon grasped that the turmoil and recklessness of Mexico City worked for Mexicans; the orderliness and decorum in Tokyo somehow worked for the Japanese.

Tokyo was also a city of books, of poets, of artists, of restaurants. The landscape of glass and steel seemed devoid of actual nature, yet I found serene and well-manicured green spaces. In the streets and clubs there were song, dance, theater, and a sea of languages. I danced one night at a salsa club in Roppongi, mingling with Peruvians, Brazilians, and the Japanese who lived among them, all of whom rattled away in Spanish or Portuguese.

To understand the Xicanx soul, which still claims facets of the Mexican soul, you have to understand *rasquache*. This term, originally from the Nahuatl language, literally means "by the seat of your pants," creativity out of disorder, doing the most with little. It's a catch-as-catch-can philosophy that is part of life, death, and everything in between.

Rasquache seemed alien to the Japanese character, which was shaped by systems, quickening social advances, and being the best, particularly in technology and finance. I learned to appreciate the great interest in Japan toward Xicanx. Xicanx chose not to totally assimilate into the mostly hollow "American" brand culture, while enriching US culture with our own art, speech, clothing, and presence. The Japanese didn't want to appropriate our culture but to honor it. The lowrider cars I saw in Tokyo came directly from LA streets—they had to be real, from the source land of Lowrider Nation.

At the core of the modern Japanese culture is a hunger for raw inventiveness and loose organization, pulsating with a creative center, not always controlled and tidy—typical of what Xicanx artists, musicians, and writers often embody. And I could also see why Xicanx artists had a fascination with the Japanese— how meticulous, organized, and original they were.

After generations of surviving inside the belly of the United States, mostly as second-class citizens, Xicanx chose the past that best defined us and strove to carve out a future that would truly embrace us. Choice was important for Japanese as well, especially after the debacle of World War II. Neither people can go back—the question at the heart of this marvelous encounter is, Which way forward?

"Despite the obvious differences," Shin Miyata said, "Chicano people are similar to Japanese. We have similar skin tones. We are small in stature. And we also love the same kind of music— mellow with *sabor*. In Japan during the 1950s, we heard the old boleros from Mexico, like Los Panchos. They used to come and play here. Similarly, Japanese kids like cholos—they feel sympathetic to them. Japanese youth are always looking to relate to things against the mainstream, against authority. This is a very strict society. There are lots of pressures to succeed. Many youth here therefore relate to Chicanos and street culture. They relate to the love of cars and how artistic and creative Chicanos have been. Japanese kids are looking for something like this in themselves. Politics is important here. They have to be against something. Japanese society tries to control kids, but many of them don't want to be controlled. That's why they love the Chicano tattoos, even the Chicano graffiti. Kids are looking for powerful, meaningful things, and some gravitate toward gangs with style. Or they gravitate to hip-hop. Or the skateboard culture."

To demonstrate this, Miyata drove me to two independent stores that sold Xicanx street-style clothing, T-shirts, CDs, and other items, including for hip-hop and skating aficionados.

Nicety was located in the Machida-shi neighborhood.

Xicanx-inspired mural art was painted over the main counter. Joker Brand clothing and other Xicanx clothing brands were on sale. Parked on the street just outside the store was a lowered 1968 Impala, owned by Rikiya Kando, the young businessman who ran Nicety.

Chiba-shi, in Chiba-ken, had one of two Wannabe's stores, owned by Masayuki Tachibana. Kousake Sakata managed the Chiba store. It had a darker street feel, with actual graffiti on the inside walls and oldies from the *East Side Story* album collection spilling out of speakers. Items included *tandos*, the small-brimmed cholo hats, bandanas, neckwear, and clothing with Mexica and Mayan motifs.

Tachibana, also known as Masa, had a shaved head, pressed baggy pants, and a long Dickies denim jacket, looking very much like an LA homeboy—he often traveled to Los Angeles to buy the latest clothing and music. Interestedly, he made a connection between cholos and the samurai, members of medieval Japanese warrior societies.

"They both represent high order and morals," Masa said. "They stand up for their communities, for others in need. They distinguish themselves with creativity, but mostly with bravery and skill."

I'm not sure how much this applied to cholos, having been one myself in my youth. But I saw the association—although for me the samurai have more to do with the Jaguar or Eagle Knights of the preconquest Mexicas, whom many present-day Xicanx activists have studied, including a version of martial arts as well as their dance, cosmology, and art. Going back to go forward makes sense.

Sakata also wore cholo-style clothing and sported an amazing array of tattoos on his arms, back, and stomach. They were done in the fine-line tattoo style and lettering that Xicanx perfected in prisons and the streets. In fact, the renowned Xicanx tattooist

Mister Cartoon (Mark Machado) inked most of Sakata's body art. Mister Cartoon, with his business partner Estevan "Scandalous" Oriol, both of whom I know, created the Joker Brand clothing enterprise; Mister Cartoon is also known for inking the amazing tattoos on recording artists such as Cypress Hill, 50 Cent, Pharrell Williams, Travis Barker of Blink-182, and Eminem.

In Tokyo, I also hooked up with Masahiro "Cholo" Wada, a Japanese radio personality on Power 046-FM in the Yamato-shi neighborhood in Kanawaga-ken who is popular among Japanese hip-hop and lowrider communities. Miyata claimed there was a growing following for such stores and radio shows in Japan.

"The future of the kids here is Chicano culture," Miyata insisted. "This is why it was important for me to bring bands like Quetzal to Japan. I wanted these kids to see and experience the deep side, the political side. So they can get the consciousness behind the music. They need to learn how to overcome struggles like Chicanos have done, and not just succumb to commercialization, to Western culture, like what's happening so much in Japan today. The Japanese kids who need to become conscious are those born in poverty, in the industrial areas. Most of them live in communities surrounding Tokyo, not so much in Tokyo, which is too expensive. They are the sons and daughters of factory workers, less educated than in Tokyo. Tokyo is more sophisticated. I think these youth need what Chicanos are about."

Xicanx can find home in Tokyo, this faraway, startling city, at least at the level of culture. Since I visited there, I've found out there are cholo/lowriding subcultures in Thailand, Taiwan, Brazil, Sweden, Amsterdam, and Spain. This seems right, especially in a world where being rootless and homeless seems to be the poignant feature of our time. If I can stand next to a lowered 1940s Ford truck with magnesium rims in Tokyo, something I could have done in East LA, and still feel the same sensation of joy that such a car can bring in both countries, then I know—it's time for borders to come down.

Of course, taking down borders is a controversial subject, especially in a time of "build that wall." There are arguments about trade and home markets and so-called terrorism used to scare residents of the most developed countries into closing in on themselves. But we have seen how divisions by race, by nation, by religion, even gangs, has led to fear and, too often, violence. I visualize a world with no borders, but also where people can be their own special kind of human being—not homogenized but driven by their own passions and geniuses—and yet still have indispensable things that bring us together.

In October 2017, Shin, Quetzal, Martha, Tex, David Gomez, and I had a reunion of sorts at the Japanese American National Museum in Little Tokyo, Los Angeles. Shin had brought a team to LA to organize a concert featuring Mexican and Japanese acts, poets, and musicians. There was even a conjunto band with Mexican-style *charro* hats, shirts, and pants. I thought they were *paisas* (two of the guys looked Mexican)—in the green room I began to address them in Spanish. One said, "No understan' . . . we Japon." They were a Japanese group that had learned the words of Mexican *corridos* in Spanish without knowing Spanish!

The last act was Quetzal and Martha with their full band. They played their original rocking and politically charged music. Then Tex Nakamura blew his powerful harmonica and added his voice to a couple of songs. And for one of their longer pieces, I came in and was able to share two poems. The LA community in attendance loved it.

So *arigato*, Japan. Or as we say in Nahuatl: *tlazhokamati*. Or in Spanish: *gracias*. Languages differ, but the sentiment is the same: thank you, Land of the Rising Sun, for opening up to me as a Xicanx poet, and for letting me savor your own magnificent heritage. "Tokyo *rifa*," as we say in the barrios of East Los Angeles, meaning "this place lives, demands respect, cannot be erased."

Con safos.

Prickly Pear Cactus: Experiencing Los Angeles with Other Eyes

"I love L.A. I can't forget its smells.
I love to make love in L.A.
It's a great city, a city without a handle,
the world's most mixed metropolis,
of intolerance and divisions.
How I love it, how I hate it . . . "

—FROM "LOVE POEM TO LOS ANGELES"

"The Big Orange"?

Los Angeles is more a prickly pear cactus than an orange, cactus being natural to the region anyway. From the early 1920s to the late 1950s, the San Fernando Valley, where I live, had up to fifteen thousand acres of a fruit the Spanish first planted in California in the 1500s. Now the orange groves are gone, replaced by single-family homes, palm tree–lined streets, strip malls, and warehouses.

Due to years of drought, in 2017, my family removed all the grass from our front yard and planted succulent plants, sage, an elderberry tree, mint, and other herbs, including the yerba santa (*Eriodictyon californicum*) used for healing by Native peoples in California for generations. And, of course, we have prickly pear cactus, which has been on the continent for at least ten thousand years.

A friend of mine living in London visited soon after the garden bloomed and took photos. I said, "Nothing much to see, dude." He gazed at me, paused, and remarked, "This is exotic where I'm from."

I suppose it would be. Los Angeles is a dreamland, popping up in Hollywood movies even when the scenes call for New York City. LA images have blown up in flicks from *Rebel Without a Cause* to *Blade Runner* to *Grease* to *The Terminator*. The Hollywood sign, as well as downtown's high-rises with their flat tops (for heliports), are known in every corner of the world. Venice, Santa Monica, or Malibu beach piers and sand get prime time on TV and in film.

I don't think of "El Lay" that way. I've lived in the parts of this City of Angels furthest removed from heaven. My story is the story of the "other" Los Angeles.

My family settled here in the mid-1950s, when I was two. We lived in Watts, an African American and Mexican ghetto/ barrio. We stayed in several homes, were evicted a few times, and were homeless for a spell during a time when my mother tried to leave my father (she ended up going back).

The house I most remember was a tiny clapboard structure on 105th Street near McKinley Avenue. My youngest sister, Gloria, was born at East LA's General Hospital when we lived there— a tiny, red-faced infant my mother brought home.

I have a much older half sister—some twenty years older— named Seni. She preceded us to Watts with a husband and two daughters (another daughter came later). They lived on 111th Street. I stayed there a couple of summers when my family departed for vacations in Mexico and left me behind (I never knew why). Soon after the Watts Rebellion of 1965, this home was torn down to make room for Locke High School—decades later I spoke there and mentioned to the students they might be sitting in my old living room!

I first attended elementary school at 109th Street School. I skipped kindergarten, since *Amá* (a shortened form of "Mamá") didn't want me in school until another sister, Ana, a year younger than me, could attend.

On my first day, I went from classroom to classroom because I couldn't speak English and teachers didn't want me among their students. A teacher finally let me stay, but she had me in a corner playing with building blocks most of the year. I'd pee in my pants since I didn't know how to say I had to go to the restroom. Whenever a Spanish word left my mouth, I was punished, including being swatted by the school's principal. I made the mistake one day of stepping into the kindergarten class my sister was in so I could pick her up. The teacher slapped me across the face in front of everyone.

And that was the better part of the day. At home, my brother José, three years older, beat the shine out of me whenever he could. He once threw me off a rooftop. Another time he dragged me around the yard with a rope around my neck. He even solicited his friends to knock me around.

Over the years José became one of the nicest guys you'd ever want to know—a hard-working, law-abiding brother, and also a wonderful husband, father, and grandfather. Unfortunately, in 2019, suffering from early Alzheimer's, he passed on at age sixty-eight.

Watts was then, and is now, the poorest neighborhood in Los Angeles. The iconic Watts Towers are here, built by Italian immigrant Simon Rodia over a thirty-three-year period. When

Rodia finished, in 1954, he left the towers in the care of a Mexican family and never returned. As a child I climbed those structures—so sturdy even rambunctious children couldn't compromise the cement, rebar, and wire mesh spirals with seventy thousand embedded pieces of porcelain, tile, and glass. Even earthquakes and man-made machines the city once used could not knock them down. Today the towers, still standing, are behind a chain-link fence in a park housing an art gallery, art studios, meeting rooms, and an outside amphitheater. In my early twenties I returned to live in Watts, and another South LA neighborhood known as Florence, with my first wife. My oldest son, Ramiro, and daughter, Andrea, were born during that time, in 1975 and 1977, respectively.

Annual Watts jazz and drum festivals have brought thousands to the park and towers. In 2015, I read poetry at one of those festivals with Ramiro, who was then forty, a kind of homecoming. Yet even with new housing and a few refurbished alleys and streets, not much has changed in Watts. Its poverty rate is over fifty percent today. It is now majority Mexican and Central American. Many African Americans in the city have been pushed out, especially after the 1965 Watts Rebellion, and even more so after the 1992 LA Uprising. This is "Riot City" after all, including the 1970 East LA Uprising—there have been more civil disturbances here in the past hundred years than any other city.

With gentrification and other displacement, much of LA's African American population and many Mexican/Central Americans are now in desert towns like Lancaster or in the "Inland Empire" (where Los Angeles, San Bernardino, and Riverside Counties meet)—or living along streets, alleys, and freeway underpasses near where they once had a home. They have been pushed out, discarded, again.

I started out in Watts, but over the years I've lived in far-flung communities in and around Los Angeles. From age eight to nineteen, I resided in the "other" valley, the San Gabriel Valley (SGV), a former fruit- and nut-growing area that by the 1960s became industrialized and suburban. Wham-O Inc., a toy company, had a factory there, as well as other assembly companies. Majority white then, the SGV was dotted with a hundred or so poor Mexican migrant communities, many named after the landscape, such as Las Lomas ("the hills," my barrio), Canta Ranas ("singing frogs"), Monte Flores ("mountain flowers"), Cherryville (for the fields the migrants worked in), or El Jardin ("the garden"). These barrios often had dirt roads, no sidewalks, abandoned cars, and goats and chickens in backyards.

In the SGV, our family first lived with Seni and her family in a two-bedroom apartment, a total of eleven of us with all the kids and adults. The children slept on blankets in the living room. Unfortunately, a family member ended up with bipolar disorder—although it wasn't called that then, and we had no idea what the hell was going on. A stabbing incident brought police to the house; the landlord evicted everyone. The two families split up, and my dad, mother, brother, two younger sisters, and I ended up in a one-bedroom squat in South San Gabriel.

When I was nine, my mother told me to find a job, because at that age she picked cotton in Texas. I took around a rusty hand-push lawn mower to my neighbors and cut their grass for 25 cents, although many yards were mostly dirt. Next I threw newspapers from a beat-up bicycle. I also cleaned well-off white people's homes and yards, and even learned to clean their swimming pools. In my teens, I packed boxes in warehouses, cleaned up at a car wash, and served as a janitor/handyman at a discount store and as a busboy in a Mexican restaurant.

These migrant communities began in the 1930s with "Okies" and "Arkies," poor whites driven from their fields due to the dust storms that ravaged their homes. By the 1940s, the communities became predominantly Mexican. When the 1960s came around, the time in which my family moved there, a uniquely organized and influential gang culture sprouted in South San Gabriel and other barrios. Called cholos, a word originally meaning "low-life Indians," Chicano gang members created the now famous fine-line, black-and-gray tattoo style and sported oversized but perfectly ironed khaki pants, long white T-shirts or Pendleton flannel shirts, and lowrider hats or beanie caps. Specialized cholo graffiti covered fences, utility poles, and underpasses. Cholos had their own way of talking, of walking, of keeping the pachuco traditions. Almost every gang from other cultures in LA has since emulated the cholo style—Bloods and Crips as well as refugee youth from El Salvador, Cambodia, or Armenia.

I was a cholo from eleven to nineteen as part of the Las Lomas street gang, using every known drug at the time, mostly heroin, as well as spending stints at three sheriff's substations, local city jails, juvenile hall, and two adult facilities. I was arrested for crimes including stealing, rioting, attempted murder, and assaulting police officers. Once, at sixteen, I spent days on "mur-derer's row" of the Hall of Justice jail in a cell next to Charles Manson (the murder charges never materialized, and I was let go). Despite my detention record, I was only ever convicted for substantially lesser charges at eighteen (for resisting arrest and drunk and disorderly conduct).

Las Lomas had one of the most violent gang wars in the 1960s and 1970s with another barrio surrounding the old San Gabriel Mission called Sangra. One of the first and biggest lowrider car clubs, Groupe, came from the unincorporated South San Gabriel community that included Las Lomas. And the Mon-gols, for a time the most violent "1 percenter" motorcycle club, who took on the Hell's Angels and other gangs, were born in the South San Gabriel/Montebello area.

As an active gang member, I got kicked out for fighting in my first year of high school and from another high school on the first day I showed up. I tried one more high school before I dropped out altogether. When I was fifteen, my parents threw me out of the house (by then we had moved to the city of San Gabriel). I slept where I could—along the LA River, or in abandoned cars, all-night movie houses, church pews, shuttered warehouses, or vacant lots. I carried a .22 handgun for protection and to mug tourists on Olvera Street (the original city pueblo) or in Chinatown.

My refuge, however, was downtown's Central Library, where writers like Ray Bradbury and Charles Bukowski had spent time. I hungered for books—my initial favorites being *Charlotte's Web*, *The Martian Chronicles*, and the black experience books of the 1960s: *The Autobiography of Malcolm X*; *Manchild in the Promised Land*, by Claude Brown; *Down These Mean Streets* by Piri Thomas; books by James Baldwin, LeRoi Jones (Amiri Baraka), Don L. Lee (Haki Madhubuti), Nikki Giovanni, and George Jackson.

I returned home after tiring of the freezing nights and abysmal situations I witnessed living in the street. My parents were livid—they didn't want me back. I didn't care. I cleared out a small room adjoined to the garage that had no running water or heat. But it had a roof.

In the garage, hidden amid boxes and piles of old clothing, I found an old Remington typewriter with stuck keys and a worn-out ribbon and began to write vignettes, thoughts, feelings. A youth organizer entered my life and became my mentor, and despite tensions between us (due to my defiance), his persistence finally got me to paint murals and became a community activist. While I still burglarized homes and shot up heroin, I also took part in Chicano movement marches, protests, and gatherings. In an agreement with this mentor, I returned to school, helped lead three school walkouts, wrote a column of my thoughts for the school newspaper, and studied revolutionary theory. I let go of the heavy drugs for a while, since I was seen as a leader and organizer. Against all odds, I caught up on lost credits and received my high school diploma even though it was too late to be part of the cap-and-gown ceremony.

For some reason I became depressed after this—perhaps feeling no one would ever see me again in that same way. I went back to heroin.

When I was eighteen, community members saved me from a long prison term for allegedly fighting with sheriff's deputies (the truth is I was trying to stop deputies from beating a hand-cuffed Chicana while she was on the ground). Teachers and neighbors wrote letters on my behalf; a few showed up in court. A judge gave me the break of a lifetime—he said he'd never seen such support for a defendant before. I ended up sentenced to time served in the county jail. I also began the process of owning my life instead of turning it over to gangs, drugs, and crime. In jail I began my first withdrawal from heroin. I was done, soul exhausted, tired of being trapped, tired of being tired. My family had given up on me. By then I'd also lost twenty-five friends to gang violence, police killings, heroin overdoses, and suicide.

I now had a vision and drive to become active—in ending barrio warfare, in establishing gang truces, and in practicing the political teachings needed to build a youth movement informed by revolutionary knowledge, organizing, and the arts—away from the vortex of violence and drugs (similar to what was happening at the same time in New York City, Chicago, Detroit, and other urban war zones).

Unlike what is generally believed, people in America's poorest communities worked hard to raise themselves up. Activists invested time and sweat equity (often with no pay) to overcome the systemic devastation overwhelming their streets, schools, and businesses, despite being undermined by police, politicians, and policy. Such leaders also contributed to ending the crack epidemic that began in LA in the early 1980s, again exploding in inner cities across the land, with complicity from government entities, gangs, and a susceptible clientele. Such brave and committed souls continue organizing till this day.

My late teens and twenties were marked by considerable instability.

After being hounded by police and sheriff's deputies due to my community activism and gang peace work and shot at by two homies (one of whom I later heard was a police informant), I snuck out of my garage room at nineteen. I found my way into a dilapidated federal housing project in San Pedro, living with and learning from revolutionary thinkers and organizers.

After a couple of months, I moved into the Mexican barrios east of the LA River, including the White Fence and Cuatro Flats neighborhoods of Boyle Heights, and Geraghty Loma in City Terrace. Over the years, I also stayed in Pasadena's Northeast 'hood when it consisted of poor Blacks and Mexicans, as well as the working-class communities of Huntington Park and Maywood.

I labored in some of the worst industrial/construction jobs— on bloody meatpacking floors, cleaning out oil and grease in massive pipes, in sewer treatment plants, as a lead foundry smelter. And I worked highly paid skilled jobs in mills and refineries.

In the middle of my twenties, I embarked in a new direction—a journalism and writing career. Myself and my second wife—a journalist and actress—moved to the Angelino Heights neighborhood, next to Echo Park, a thriving Mexican/Central American area whose residents have now been largely displaced by high-end development.

When my new wife left after a mere six months, I moved in with another woman and later bought my first home with her in Highland Park, a strong Mexican community. I remember walking from Avenue 57 to York Boulevard among *panaderías*, botanicas, and taquerias. Now, thirty years later, it is another highly gentrified community with boutiques, cafes, and juice bars. In recent years, a homeless enclave has sprung up nearby in a plant-infested area of the LA River, consisting of former Highland Park residents.

After two years, I broke up with my live-in partner and returned to Boyle Heights. I moved into a house owned by my brother José, who worked as a phone installer and lived with his second wife and their two daughters. For everything we went through when I was a child, I'm grateful for my brother for being there when I most needed him.

The next big turn was in 1985, just before I turned thirty-one—I moved to Chicago. There I got together with my last and greatest love, Trini. After three years of dating and living together, we married in 1988. By 1994 we had two boys, Ruben and Luis (also known as Chito). Trini also helped me raise Ramiro and Andrea. After Ramiro got into trouble with gangs, crime, and prison, I wanted to push him away, but I couldn't. We held on tight as he took us on a roller coaster through hell.

At the same time, I helped create urban peace and youth empowerment organizations in Chicago like Youth Struggling for Survival, the Increase the Peace network, and Humboldt Park's Teen Reach.

Although Trini and I had bought our first house together in Chicago's Logan Square, by 2000 we moved back to Los Angeles. This was mostly to keep our young sons away from the entrapments that held their older brother. We couldn't lose any more boys. Andrea and her daughter, Catalina, later joined us in LA.

Trini grew up in the ghetto/barrio of Pacoima in the northeast San Fernando Valley. Once known as the "Mexican" side of the Valley, it's now majority Mexican and Central American, with a significant, although declining, African American population. Today Pacoima, with a population of one hundred thousand, has around a 50 percent unemployment rate, federal housing projects, and gangs. At the elementary school Trini attended (as did my son Chito), 25 percent of students are homeless. Interestingly, Trini's large Mexican family of eleven children never got involved in gangs or drugs despite the environment. We wanted to be close to this amazing family—there were now tons of nephews and nieces. We lived in Pacoima for six months before buying a house in the two-square-mile city called San Fernando, surrounded by the Los Angeles communities of Pacoima, Mission Hills, and Sylmar.

In 2001, Trini and I helped establish Tia Chucha's Café Cultural and Bookstore in the Sylmar community (now a nonprofit called Tia Chucha's Centro Cultural). At the time there were no bookstores, movie houses, or comprehensive arts spaces in the northeast San Fernando Valley, home to half a million people.

Tia Chucha's also sponsored annual concerts for a few years at the John Anson Ford Amphitheater, which brought Cheech Marin, La Santa Cecilia, Tierra, Ceci Bastida, and many other Mexican/Xicanx performers, but also African American, Filipino, and Japanese American performers. Once, Charles Wright and the Watts 103rd Street Rhythm Band (famous for 1960s hits "Express Yourself" and "Love Land") played there.

These concerts were organized by the singer/performer/activist Rubén "Funkahuatl" Guevara, who fronted Ruben and the Jets in the 1970s and Con Safos in the 1980s. In 2017 Ruben published a memoir, *Confessions of a Radical Chicano Doo-Wop Singer* (University of California Press).

Ruben even directed the staged production of my one-man poem/play, "Notes of a Bald Cricket," at the John Anson Ford Theater to a full house. To my surprise, Annette Bening showed up with her teen daughter, who had read *Always Running* for her high school English class and wanted to say hello.

After almost twenty years, Tia Chucha's serves upwards of eighteen thousand people a year. We have classes in music, guitar, keyboards, and drumming, as well as *son jarocho*. We have writing, theater, mural painting, and other arts workshops. We've taught Nahuatl language and Mexicayotl (indigenous cosmology) classes. A Mexica *danza* group, Temachtia Quetzalcoatl, provides workshops and ceremony. We have a youth empowerment program, the Young Warriors. We also created Trauma to Transformation, working with incarcerated men and women, the formerly incarcerated, and families of the incarcerated with writing, theater, and visual arts. And we host the only annual outdoor literacy and arts festival in the San Fernando Valley, Celebrating Words: Written, Performed and Sung.

In the fall of 2014, I was designated as the official poet laureate of Los Angeles. The press conference to announce this appointment was held in the Central Library, next to those very shelves I once wandered past as a lost, drug-addicted gang youth—shelves that now hold many of my published poetry, fiction, nonfiction, and children's books.

When Ramiro moved in with the family, he brought much needed positivity and genuine heart. My son Ruben graduated from UCLA, magna cum laude. My youngest son, Chito, is writing stories and scripts, and carving out a creative path for himself. Andrea is back in Chicago, with a five-year-old son, Jack Carlos. And my granddaughter Catalina, who as of this writing is twenty-three, graduated in 2018 from Bennington

College in Vermont and is now in the master's program in poetry at Rutgers University of New Jersey.

As the Diné say, I'm walking among beauty and blessings.

If you go to the San Gabriel Valley now, you'll notice the Chinese, Korean, Vietnamese, or Japanese lettering on top of buildings and strip malls. The SGV now has the largest Asian population in the United States. Most of the white people have left the area. Many of the Mexican migrant housing structures were razed. Mansions and townhouses, for a while, were being built next to small wood-frame shacks. This process began around the mid-1980s—a sort of gentrification, since this involved people with money, not the poorer Asian immigrants from Cambodia or Laos.

There's a park in Monterey Park called La Loma. White residents once chased me out of there when I was eight years old. Even though there was no official sign saying so, Mexicans were apparently not welcome. A few years ago, at the invitation of my friend, former *Los Angeles Times* reporter Jesse Katz, I threw out the first baseball for a new Little League organization at La Loma Park, with teams consisting primarily of Asians and Mexicans.

Then, in 2017, a Luis J. Rodriguez Reading Park was created at the Sanchez Elementary School in Rosemead. I attended that school when it was part of the blighted South San Gabriel neighborhood. Poverty, gangs, even human trafficking of girls, often through motels along Garvey Avenue, permeated the area in those times.

Now the homes there are larger and stuccoed. Dirt roads have been paved. The school looks clean and modern. The day of the dedication I talked to the children, who were mostly Asian, though sprinkled here and there were Mexican indigenous faces. I was a sorry-ass student—shy, bullied, awkward. I joined a gang, and everything changed. It was unimaginable to me as a child that I'd return in my sixties to celebrate this space with my name on it.

Los Angeles is in deep transition. Its 469 square miles traverse deserts, beaches, wooded mountains (with snow in the winter), and dense urban communities (South Central LA is the country's most overcrowded area). The city is an increasing cost-of-living miscreation, having seen a 32 percent rise in rents since 2000. It has the lowest home ownership rate of a major metropolitan area in the country. The county has the largest homeless street population—around fifty-eight thousand people—while 58 billionaires reside in the city's richest zip codes. The inequalities here are dismal, and they're spreading.

Since my return to Los Angeles I've taken friends, guests, and journalists from around the United States as well as England, Italy, Brazil, Japan, and Australia, including TV news crews and TV writers, on what Ramiro calls "the cholo tour"—no beaches, Hollywood trappings, or Disneyland. I take them to the "other" LA—to places I've laid my head, where there are people on the streets, all kinds of violence and poverty, but also life, murals, poetry. These places don't exist on tourist maps. The visitors are amazed by how much character there is—by how disheveled some of the streets appear, but also by the wonderful smells, sounds, and sights of Mexican food, auto shops, and children's laughter. They gawk at the old brick buildings and Victorian structures that pop up here and there. And even if the homes are small and wood framed, they are mostly clean and alive with color, with flowerpots and, at times, stalks of corn and chicken coops.

One TV crew from Europe wanted me to show them gang members. I said I don't do that. They were disappointed, but what they saw was eye-opening just the same. Ironically, as we sat at a taco stand to take a break, a gang shootout exploded across the street. One dude ran up to a car and began firing into it. The car sped off. It was fast and furious. In fact, the TV crew was so busy eating and talking they didn't even think to look up. I didn't say anything.

This is the Los Angeles where Santa Ana winds scatter dry leaves, and droughts make tinder out of the formerly green brush. Where wildfires are metaphor and reality for our internal and external terrains. Where the city is music but also muscles, a rain dance often with no rain, neon glare and smog-tinged skyline, held together in a spiderweb of freeways. It's a place where even jacarandas and palm trees are transplants.

This is where the city's buildings are bricked and nailed together with survival stories, war stories, and love stories—the kind of harrowing accounts Los Angeles unfurls at three a.m., when ghosts meander along the upturned pavement or rumble by on vintage cars, and all-night diners convert into summits for the played out, heartsick, and suicidal.

There's a migrant soul in this rooted city: Skid Row next to the Diamond District, waves of foam against barnacled piers, cafes and boutiques next to *botanicas*. Ravines and gulleys turn into barrios, rustic homes with gardens dot bleak cityscapes, and suburbs burst with world-class graffiti.

Fragmented yet cohesive, Los Angeles demands reflection on ourselves and the unstable ground we call home, where people die for lack of a roof or food or compassion. As renowned LA writer John Fante would say, these persons are "songs over sidewalks," imaginations on the interchange, humanity that deserves connection, touch, breath. These roads, bridges, and alleys also contain concertos. Breezes over the ocean's darkest depths are replete with harmonies, and a howling moon and red sunset serve as backdrops for every aching interlude.

Los Angeles is where every step rhymes, where languages flit off tongues like bows across strings, skateboarders and aerosol spray cans clatter in a daily percussion, and even angels intone "We can do better," while haggling at garage sales.

Monsters of Our Own Making

"I can't see 'em coming down my eye
so I had to make this poem cry
this pen bleed
this paper scream with emotions with hopes it
   makes
us free . . . "

—JIMMY MCMILLAN, POET INCARCERATED AT A
CALIFORNIA STATE PRISON

A lifer stood up to read his writing after fifteen weeks of sitting in a creative writing class I facilitated at a classroom in a maximum-security yard of Lancaster State Prison (California State Prison, Los Angeles County). It was our last day of that session. I had just passed out completion certificates and was about to share juice and cake the prison kitchen staff had brought us. The forty-something-year-old man hadn't said much during the previous weeks. He didn't seem to be writing either. I had noticed this, but it didn't bother me. The class was lively with a flow of ideas and expressions; most of the guys were serving life sentences, some without the possibility of parole (LWOP).

I always feel people listen in their own way. Seeds were being planted, and if someone kept coming to class, I kept teaching.

But now this man stood up and read, opened up his heart

about how, ever since he could remember, he had been abused; how drugs took his parents away from him; how he bounced around in the foster-care system, juvenile detention centers, and prison; and how being callous, a predator, had given him power, identity, a way of getting back. But he also related how lost he had become—detached, not fully human. His words were not a litany of excuses or complaints. They were recognition of terrible choices he'd made in a world of limited choices, of the fears and paralysis that impelled him to diminish his true callings.

This OG, who was African American, didn't care how he would be perceived at that moment. Tears began to fall from his eyes, even as his voice remained strong. We were all riveted—crying tears inside if not on the outside. The men's silence was the best mark of respect he could have received. When he was done, the quiet lingered for a beat, then the applause rushed in. The men were visibly moved as this man stood poised, unwavering, in the whirl of dark and convoluted sentiments. This and similar moments have made my work in prisons some of the most healing and sacred anywhere.

I've been coming into prisons to lead workshops, healing circles, talks, and poetry readings for forty years. I've done this work in prisons all over California (San Quentin, Soledad, New Folsom, Chino, and Lancaster) as well as county and city jails, and juvenile lockups up and down the state. I've also entered prisons, jails, and juvenile facilities in Illinois, Michigan, Pennsylvania, Connecticut, Indiana, Ohio, Nebraska, North Carolina, Texas, New Mexico, Arizona, Nevada, Washington, Virginia, Louisiana, and Delaware. I've worked with organizations like Barrios Unidos, the William James Foundation, Insight-Out, InsideOUT Writers, and as an employee of the Alliance for California Traditional Arts.

This work has gone global. Over the years, I've visited ten adult prisons and a juvenile facility in El Salvador; two prisons in Guatemala; two prisons in Nicaragua; a prison and juvenile hall in the state of Chihuahua, Mexico; five prisons in Argentina; and a young adult lockup in southern England, and met with juvenile offenders in Italy outside of their facility.

Most of these visits were one-time talks or readings, although I did spend three days in that prison in England, several continuous weeks in Chino Prison, and eight months in Lancaster Prison in 2007; and beginning in the fall of 2016, I conducted several thirteen- to seventeen-week classes at the latter.

I see prisons as the shadows of the "normal" world, mirroring the fragile economic, political, and cultural foundations we've stood on for over 240 years as a country, based on slavery, inequality, and the interplay between the powerful and powerless. Prisons are also places of light and intelligence within the dark. Any idealization that prisons or the police state are the answers to crime, dysfunction, or "evil" is naïve and strangely cynical. Naïveté and cynicism may seem a dichotomy, but they are also interrelated.

Two dangers in this country are to be naïve about what made us, what we face, and where we're going and to be cynical—tired, negative, perpetually sabotaging hope with an attitude of "Why bother?" Prisons *persist* because of the interweaving of the naïve and cynical. But they *exist* because the people this society cannot feed, house, teach, or incorporate must be put somewhere. If these people won't go to war, stay employed, or otherwise contribute to the "system," then dysfunction and crime are inevitable, and prisons are the perfect industry to feed off the "monsters" among us.

They are, however, monsters of our own making.

People aren't born to steal, lie, hurt, or kill. Yet with enough external and internal pressures, you can mold such a person. Anyone is capable. Just deprive people of basic needs, especially of healthy nurturing—rampant among the poor—and of viable ways to go. Put such persons into an "oven," as a homie used to say, and you're more likely to bake a gang member, a thief, a murderer. The point is that our society—our culture and its frazzled webbing—makes crime and criminals not just possible but predictable.

I'm not against personal accountability—I've had to address this with countless men, women, and youth over the years, beginning with myself and with my oldest son Ramiro, who is now gang free, drug free, and crime free. But personal accountability works best if we also comprehend the familial, economic, and political forces at play.

Of course, there are people who are more capable of resisting the pressures of duress, depravity, and disinterest with enough soul depth, intelligence, and creativity. It helps if they have strong moral and character development along the way. I witness this in prisons all the time. But, again, the chances are that for most people, certain circumstances will most likely lead to certain results.

Most of our society treats people as if they are static beings— once in trouble, always in trouble. It's as if we believe that once a person is inclined to pathological levels of lying, manipulating, and cheating, even violence, there is no breaking the mold. Prison's main premise is punishment. We punish those who have broken the rules, and we believe that doing so will serve as a deterrent to others, who will, as the thinking goes, do whatever they can to avoid such punishment.

But punishment only works up to a certain point, particularly in a child's development, and only if the punishment fits the "crime." It doesn't work for those who've been "punished" just for being—in black or brown skins, migrants from other countries, working class, poor, a woman, or LGBTQ. These are circumstances not of one's choosing. It's among youth in these circumstances where discrimination and the organized blocking of decent and meaningful work, health care, education, and support in the complete flowering of one's development and unique contributions can do the most damage.

As my wife Trini says, it's about "the poverty of access."

Trini's words inspired a poem by African American poet and northeast San Fernando Valley resident Jeffery Martin:

"The Poverty of Access"

It cheats a long line of tired, withered hands
coursing through generation after generation
of veins too weary to imagine
a kinder existence

It cheats brilliant minds
it cheats brilliant minds
it cheats brilliant minds
leaving them suffocating on a frustration
they can no longer define

It cheats limber bodies
that have no idea
they were meant to dance

dance in the four directions of life
meshing with the deities of
wind fire earth and water
creating light bright
and transforming

The poverty of access
closes books before sentences are complete
before action can coincide with thought
before the mind body and spirit
introduce themselves

This poverty is harshest amongst its young
for it starves them intellectually
long before ravaging their stomachs

It says no you can't and means it
it says you are unworthy
and means it
it says here is where you belong
and means it

The poverty of access
steals souls as well as land
murders ambition as well as men and women
who ask too many questions
it fills prisons and dungeons
with corpses breathing yet
breathless

moving yet motionless
eating yet starved

It gives prostitution its place
then sneers
it gives violence its place
then sneers
it gives homelessness its place
then sneers

it gives crime its place
and then claims prophecy

This poverty of access
does not tell stories
it stunts them

with nasty words like
cannot
will not
must not

It is a poverty that guarantees
an outcome as unfair
as it is unwarranted

Under these realities, there's little or no deterrence to crime because prisons (or foster care or mental health facilities or you name the institution created to supposedly address the gaps) become a rite of passage, part of the "outlaw" life, the outsider reality, that such people get driven into. The cumulative traumas create a vortex of emotional and pathological anguish that sucks out all the enjoyment and hope one would otherwise have in life. Looking at it this way, going to prison, taking drugs, or being in a gang can be rational decisions.

The same can be said of mass incarceration in the United States, whose net was widened with "three-strikes" laws and the practices of "truth in sentencing," gang and gun enhancements, trying youth as adults, and more. Of course people driven to the brink will fall through the cracks—maybe not all of them, but enough of them.

We make more laws and end up with more lawlessness.

Mass incarceration is this country's chief strategy to address poverty, especially targeted against those on the desperate edge of survival and in the grip of the discontent related to poverty. Without ways to get rid of poverty, prison is society's answer—and as others have pointed out, through prisons we maintain a system of slavery.

In California, the most affected are people of color—African Americans, Mexicans/Central Americans, Asians, and Native Americans. But poor whites are not exempt. In the state of California, with a $12 billion annual budget, prisons have become the largest form of subsidized poor peoples' housing. The yearly cost per prisoner in the state is $64,000. Disproportionately, those prisoners are black and brown people: more than 70 percent of the state's prison population is African American or Chicano/Mexican/Central American (42 percent brown people, 29 percent black), although together they are little more than 45 percent of the state's total population.

It's time for real freedom in this country—not just the freedom to speak out, to write, or to assemble but ultimately freedom from want, hunger, lack of decent homes, and repression. It's time to stop making criminals of circumstance.

Humans are capable of great transcendence—able to go beyond material, and often man-made, constraints. We can become vessels for the unseen, with the power to overcome actual prisons but also prisons of mind and soul that chain our capacities. Reconnection, realignment, and rethinking are part of the process, albeit often arduous, long, and full of setbacks. But with this process, success is a likely outcome.

Today most people have forgotten this. We've forgotten the process needed whenever anyone or anything goes awry, overcome by social, familial, and personal failings. When people feel these skewed energies running through them, too often they are impelled in their very bones to great destruction, against themselves or others.

Today activists are establishing restorative and transformative justice practices as alternatives to punishment-based models. In such practices, agreements are made between perpetrators and victims to restore whatever was taken, hurt, or damaged. In the process one also gives back from one's own gifts—that's real restitution, not cleaning streets or paying into "victim" accounts. Both parties are transformed. Whenever a perpetrator is healed, community is healed, and a new basis is laid for more healing. When enacted comprehensively, rightly resourced, and given enough time and patience, these methods almost always work.

However, today most prisons often end up making sophisticated criminals of these same perpetrators rather than redeeming them—all at taxpayers' expense.

Of course, there are strong and powerful exceptions. And these men and women prove that change is everywhere; change is the way of spirit and nature. Change is God's plan—and this has been proven by millions of people.

In the last twenty-six years I've entered a number of *penales* in El Salvador: Mariona, San Vicente, Ciudad Barrios, Zacatecoluca, Chalatenango, Cojutepeque, Quezaltepeque, Izalco, and San Francisco Gotera. This is a country that knows about prisons. As of June 2017, El Salvador had an imprisonment rate of 590 per 100,000. Around 38,410 people were incarcerated (not counting youth or young adults), and 3,000 more were in holding tanks, out of a total population of 6.5 million. The imprisonment rate in the United States, which has the highest rate of all developed countries, is 478 per 100,000.

The facilities I visited were stark and indefensible. Some had no electricity or clean water. Diseases were rampant, with little or no medical care available. In larger facilities that held mostly men, separate cells contained young mothers holding babies, who were also behind bars with them. Housing was extremely overcrowded, with cells built for four men now holding twenty. One facility had layers of dungeons with decreasing sunlight as one continued deeper below ground. There were separate prisons for Mara Salvatrucha-13 and 18th Street members, as well as for prisoners not affiliated with those gangs.

I also visited women-only institutions with cellblocks loaded with beds, clothing, blankets, and whatever possessions they could get a hold of, including *chambitas*, makeshift housing on the prison yard. In many institutions the only food prisoners had was what their families could bring.

No human being should be treated this way. But the prisoners here are *maras* (Central American slang for gang members), and the narrative that drives this cruelty asserts they're nothing more than stone-cold killers, torturers, and extortionists of the poor. It declares they are unredeemable, that they *deserve* this treatment—or worse.

These *maras* only exist because of civil wars, driven by money and power, during which the United States, especially in the Reagan years, escalated each conflict by supporting the ruthless families and governments that ran things at the expense of the vast majority of mostly indigenous or *campesino* people.

Wars to stop "communism," in the 1950s through the 1980s, claimed a hundred thousand lives in Nicaragua, seventy-five thousand lives in El Salvador, two hundred thousand lives in Guatemala, and thousands more in the Contra War from 1981 to 1990 in Honduras and Nicaragua. In the 1980s, some three million refugees from these countries ended up in the United States, the majority coming to Los Angeles, but also Houston, Washington, DC, Long Island, or San Francisco.

Tragically, in Los Angeles, the trauma of civil war and death squads met the trauma of inner-city Chicano and African American gangs. Many Salvadoran and other Central American children of these refugees joined Chicano gangs that had existed, in some cases, since the turn of the last century—or from the 1960s, like 18th Street.

Mara Salvatrucha, on the other hand, was created by Salvadoran refugee youth in the early 1980s. First they were known as Mara Stoners—a metal-rock loving, long-haired, AC/DC T-shirt–wearing party crew. After some ended up in juvenile hall and LA County youth probation camps, they returned to their homes as cholos and took on the "Salvatrucha" tag. They originally became part of 18th Street, but later broke off and waged war against 18th Street and other gangs in the Pico-Union barrio as well as their Koreatown, East Hollywood, Northeast San Fernando, and South LA neighborhoods.

Street-gang life overall in the United States reached its highest levels of violence during this time. In Los Angeles, one estimate was that more than ten thousand young people were killed from 1980 to 2000, propelled by the drug trade but also by turf battles. The majority of those killed or arrested were Chicanos and African Americans, but Central Americans were also among them.

After the 1992 LA Uprising, which left sixty-three people dead and a billion dollars in property damage, US immigration officials targeted Mexican and Central American gang members for deportation while law enforcement agencies moved to lock up more US-born black and Chicano youth, helping create the largest mass incarceration system in the country.

By 1993, the Mara Salvatrucha—which by then also incorporated Guatemalan, Honduran, and Mexican refugee youth— joined the largely Chicano *Sureño* gang structure, which was when they added the number 13 to their name. What most news reports fail to point out is that almost all LA-based Latino gangs have "13" after their name, including the gang in my barrio, Lomas 13.

Despite the manufactured notoriety, MS-13 is only one of LA's five hundred or so Latino gangs. While the federal government claims there are ten thousand MS-13 members in the United States (which I highly doubt), this is still only 1 percent of the million or so gang members around the country. Remember, there are still active super-gang alliances spread around the country—including the LA-based Bloods and Crips (mostly African Americans), *Sureños* and *Norteños* (Southern California or Northern California Mexicans), and Chicago-based Folk and People (including the Latin Kings, Gangster Disciples, Vice Lords, Latin Maniac Disciples, and hundreds more). And there are also white supremacist criminal gangs in the streets and prisons that, per capita, have probably committed more violence than any other group.

And while Trump claims that MS-13 is amassing at the border, in 2018, MS-13 members were only .096 percent of the migrants ICE detained there. MS-13 may be *gruesos* (hardcore), but they are not the worst or largest US street gang.

All this talk about MS-13 fits into a false narrative—that undocumented criminals are causing most of the terror and violence in the United States. With this deceit as cover, thousands of LA-based gang youth, along with other so-called criminals, were deported. By 1996, under the Clinton administration, a new immigration law targeted convicted people without proper immigration documents, even for minor, nonviolent crimes. Upwards of a million people have been returned to their countries of origin since then. The greatest number of deportees ended up in Mexico and Central America, although other countries like Cambodia and Armenia also saw an influx of sophisticated US-trained criminals.

In Central America, these deportations changed a culture. MS-13 and 18th Street—heavily tattooed like their Chicano counterparts, dressed in cholo attire, and talking in the street lingo of LA's barrios, but also now trained in urban gang warfare and extortion tactics—brought all their disputes to the Northern Triangle countries of El Salvador, Guatemala, and Honduras, as well as parts of Mexico. In Belize, gang deportees were mostly Bloods and Crips. This created more violence in these places, which in many cases exceeded that of their civil wars.

People in these countries had long understood class wars— battles between those who owned land and those who didn't, the Right and the Left—but not *this*: drive-by or walk-by shootings, whole families targeted just because of which gang one family member belonged to, or didn't. Nobody understood killing because of *letras* (letters) such as MS or *numeros* (numbers) such as 18th Street.

This is the madness of exporting US-based barrio warfare.

The US government delivered these gangs to countries with few or no resources, with slums that crawled up hillsides and in concentric circles around capital cities, without work or opportunities, with gaping gulfs between those who have and those who don't—countries that for decades suffered through massacres, death squads, beheadings, tortures, and disappearances, layer upon layer of grinding, crushing violence.

The gang violence in these countries can be horrendous: Grenade attacks. Cut-up bodies. Mothers and fathers and siblings slaughtered. Now, some MS-13 and 18th Street members have returned to the United States, most with this degree of violence under their belt, and have spread out to cities across the nation, in a vicious cycle created and perpetuated by the United States government.

Despite this, the United States refuses to take responsibility. Instead, Trump and other Republicans cynically use the mess they set up in the Northern Triangle—as well as the thousands of migrants at the border escaping its violence—to consolidate their power.

Here's a truth that's often missed: these gang youth can be helped. I know this based on gang intervention work throughout the United States and across borders, based on my own forty-five years of work in prevention, intervention, and urban peace. I know of transformative and healing work done with MS-13 as well as Chicano gangs to get them out of *la vida loca* ("the crazy life") and into treatment, jobs, schooling, and families. Like any gang member, MS-13 and 18th Street members can be rehabilitated, retrained, and reincorporated into society on a positive and healthy basis. Organizations like Homies Unidos, Homeboy Industries, and Barrios Unidos have already proven this for some time. This is what we should have done with MS-13 and 18th Street youth instead of deporting them, wreaking havoc instead of weaving hope.

The mass media, LAPD, and federal authorities instead have focused on MS-13 as if they are an isolate from another planet, another species of gang. MS-13 became the first street gang designated as a transnational terrorist organization. In September 2017, Congress approved a law targeting these so-called "immigrant" gangs as the "worst of the worst." But those in the street or in prison, and gang interventionists working with them, know they are capable of profound and lasting transformations.

I first visited El Salvador with Donna DeCesare, a New York–based award-winning photojournalist. In 1993, we received a Dorothea Lange–Paul Taylor Prize from the Center for Documentary Studies at Duke University to research, do interviews, and photograph *maras* in Los Angeles and El Salvador.

We also spoke at the Salvadoran Youth Confronting Violence conference in 1996, organized by nongovernmental agencies from Italy and other European countries, which led to perhaps the first MS-13 and 18th Street peace efforts.

Donna and I helped bring members from both gangs to address their concerns, including youth with *placasos* (gang monikers) such as Diablo, Crazy Eyes, Pelón, Villain, Negro, and Whisper. At the conference, gang leaders, mayors of major cities, and members of the new National Police signed a peace accord. In the end, MS-13 and 18th Street members embraced each other, as did priests and evangelical ministers (who were also in conflict) and National Police officers and community members.

But the political will to sustain the peace was not there. The Salvadoran government, led at the time by the right-wing ARENA party, undermined the peace and, a few years later, instituted "Mano Dura" ("Iron Fist") and "Super Mano Dura" policies against the *maras*. The US government provided $3 billion from 2008 to 2017 for these efforts, mostly for the growing private-security industry (with investments from US-based companies) and new policing and prison strategies under the Central America Regional Security Initiative (CARSI).

Despite this, another powerful opportunity surfaced for peace when MS-13 and 18th Street (also known as Barrio 18) in 2012 established a truce in one of the major prisons, which spread out to other prisons and into major areas of the country.

That year, I returned to El Salvador with ten urban peace leaders, advocates, and researchers from LA, San Francisco, New York City, Washington, DC, and London—a team coordinated by Luis Cardona, a Puerto Rican/Guatemalan former Latin King and peace warrior in Montgomery County, Maryland. Known as the Transnational Advisory Group in Support of the Peace Process in El Salvador (TAGSPPES), our main charges were to assess, assist, and advise the growing peace movement.

A Salvadoran priest and an activist aided these efforts: Monsignor Fabio Colindres and former guerilla leader Raúl Mijango. The peace echoed the End Barrio Warfare Coalition and other peace efforts of Chicanos in the 1970s in California as well as Bloods and Crips truces of the 1990s. Necessarily, it also had its own unique Salvadoran qualities, based on the peace accords in 1992 that officially ended twelve years of civil war.

The results were extraordinary. In some places, there was a 70 percent drop in violence; murders declined from fourteen per day to five. The peace included highly publicized turning over of firearms and the end of many extortion rings. Around twelve Peace and Security Zones (Zonas de Paz y Seguridad) were introduced where gang members worked with community members to garden, learn trades, and paint murals without being attacked. I introduced the latter concept from the Peace Zones I worked with in Chicago in the 1990s among the predominantly Mexican and Puerto Rican communities of Humboldt Park, Logan Square, Pilsen, and Little Village.

During this trip, the TAGSPPES team visited six Salvadoran prisons, including one for women and a juvenile detention facility. We met with MS-13 and Barrio 18 peace leaders. We talked to community organizers in various pro-youth organizations and dialogued with government officials. By then, the left-wing FMLN had a president and other officials in public office. Unfortunately, political pressure from the United States, among other internal pressures, ended up *again* pulling the plug on peace.

In 2013, the Organization of American States (OAS) invited me to San Salvador to speak at a gang conference. However,

TAGSPPES members were told not to mention the gang peace or the United States would remove its share of funds, in the millions, from the Washington, DC–based organization. We were able to address best practices in gang prevention and intervention, all of which was valuable. But we were silenced on what was potentially the most powerful path to peace—gang members giving up arms and crime in return for a real process to alleviate job insecurity, derelict housing, and lack of education.

In addition, El Salvador needed strategic structural, economic, and political changes. This peace had to improve life for the whole country, not just for gang members. Providing resources only to gang members wouldn't work in a place with few or no jobs for most people. A firm economic basis was needed for healthy, stable, and long-range peace for everyone. Yet peace between gangs—as with the earlier truces between Bloods and Crips or between Chicano gangs in California—could have been the catalyst for such structural changes.

That was an objective the Salvadoran government, as well as US hemispheric interests, could have achieved. Instead, in El Salvador and in the United States, such peace was disrupted by government suppression, which inevitably caused gangs to become entrenched and intractable. The government eventually imprisoned Raúl Mijango. Gangs faced more prisons and police, but little aid to end poverty, or for drug treatment, jobs retraining, healthy reentry into communities, and transformative justice.

Even former New York City mayor Rudy Giuliani got into the act. In 2015, his private-security firm ended up in El Salvador, and was paid millions of dollars for its services, even though Giuliani oversaw the rise of racial profiling, police abuses, and the increased shootings of unarmed people in the African American, Puerto Rican, and Dominican communities of New York. Invited by the Salvadoran National Association of

Private Enterprise (ANEP), Giuliani was quoted in news services as saying that MS-13 and Barrio 18 had to be "annihilated." Lest this be confused as a metaphor, while visiting Guatemala, Giuliani reportedly told his hosts, "You are not going to solve [crime with] schools, libraries, nice neighborhoods, and sports teams. You have to emphasize law enforcement."

Again, by 2017, President Donald Trump and then–US attorney general Jeff Sessions were throwing around Giuliani's same language and advocating similar actions against the *maras*. Giuliani and others benefited financially from the Central American gang crisis while simultaneously making things worse. They also worked to deflect attention from US culpability for the high levels of disarray and disruption in El Salvador—the real source of the violence and crime.

Today killings in the Northern Triangle are more frequent than anywhere in the world: El Salvador has the worst murder rate, while Honduras is second and Guatemala third. Only parts of Mexico caught in drug-cartel wars, and war zones like Syria, have worse levels of violence. This extraordinary violence fueled a new migration crisis between 2013 and 2015, when some one hundred thousand unaccompanied minors fled the Northern Triangle to the United States; their exodus in turn fueled the crisis from 2018 to the present of the appalling treatment of asylum seekers along the border.

I first entered a prison to assist in creative-writing workshops in 1980. The facilitator was the late Manuel "Manazar" Gamboa, a Xicanx poet, formerly incarcerated (seventeen years) ex-heroin addict, former pachuco (from the Bishop barrio of the old Chavez Ravine neighborhood that was razed in the 1950s to build Dodger Stadium), and renowned community activist.

At the time, I was a daily newspaper reporter for the *San*

Bernardino Sun. But I had known Manazar since the late 1970s, when we both took part in the Los Angeles Latino Writers Association. In the early eighties, Manazar and I, along with others in the community, founded Galería Ocaso, a Chicano-oriented art gallery and performance space in the Echo Park barrio. I was its poetry curator.

At Chino Prison's writing workshops, prisoners came away having created incredible work—poems, essays, and stories. Manazar became my mentor in this area as I watched how the men opened up, dug deep, and shared in his workshops. They even had a feral cat on the main yard they named Chino Louie, supposedly after me.

One dude whose work blew me away was John Dominguez, known as "Bandit," from Watts. He had done twenty-three years in California prisons, mostly for the sale and use of heroin, and was due to be released. I decided to write a long personal essay on Bandit for the *San Bernardino Sun.* I entered the prison with permission, accompanied by a photographer, and followed Bandit around.

After his release, I went to the sober-living home he was in and witnessed his struggles to find a job and establish meaningful interactions, and his frustration trying to be a father to a daughter he hardly knew. Bandit ended up sabotaging his time "back in the world" by using heroin again.

The last time I saw Bandit he was in a holding tank at the LA County Men's Central Jail. It was 1981, and Bandit had only been out of prison for six months. He was now awaiting transfer to state prison for parole violations. Bandit explained how his parole officer, a younger man, disrespected him, even humiliated him, saying he was an ex-con with no future. The only job he could get was cleaning around a machine shop: little pay, little joy.

With calmness in his voice and a resigned expression on his face, Bandit told me, "Free is not free . . . All I know is prison, and in prison the familiar is more comforting and stable than the uncertainties of being 'free.'"

Bandit explained how in prison he had clear routines, housing, and three meals a day. Even if this existence was limited, back "in the world," it was one painful battle after another, including facing a cold-hearted parole officer who appeared to do everything in his power to encourage Bandit to fail. He got tired of fighting those battles real quick. Bandit needed help, treatment—but for the poorest people, prison is the only treatment they get.

After more than two decades being institutionalized behind bars, Bandit did what he could to return to the one comfort he understood—a prison cell.

In the summer of 2010, I spent two weeks in Manchester and London, England, speaking at universities, high schools, and community centers, primarily in Afro-Caribbean communities. Josephine Metcalf, a researcher, writer, and university professor, hosted me along with Barbara Becnel, who coauthored several books by former Crips leader Stanley "Tookie" Williams, including *Blue Rage, Black Redemption.*

Despite an international outcry, Governor Arnold Schwarzenegger had Tookie executed in 2005, after he spent more than twenty-five years on death row for four murders, although Tookie had renounced his former life and did more to convince youth to leave gangs than Schwarzenegger would ever do.

As for Josephine, she later wrote the 2012 book *The Culture and Politics of Contemporary Street Gang Memoirs*, which studied the impact of my book *Always Running*, among others.

My friend Garth Cartwright, a London-based music writer, also showed me around London. Garth's book *More Miles Than Money:*

Journeys Through American Music had a chapter on East LA that featured an interview with me, along with photos. He arranged a slot on Robert Elms's BBC Radio London radio show and a poetry reading in the Darbuka Club, a popular London club.

On top of this, Josephine set up three days of workshops at Her Majesty's Young Offenders Institution in Portland, on the southern coast. This prison housed convicts aged eighteen to twenty-one. I was impressed with the available programming, including a radio station, horses, gardens, and vocational training. But problems have been reported with inmates being locked up for twenty-one hours a day and rampant violence against staff and prisoners.

Before I showed up, prisoners were informed I was "Mexican," an ethnicity they had never seen before (Colombians, Peruvians, and other Latinx live in England, but few Mexicans). Yet they knew a lot about Mexican drug cartels. At the time, Sinaloa Cartel leader Joaquín "El Chapo" Guzmán had escaped from prison and become the world's most wanted fugitive. The first question the prisoners asked me was, "Where's El Chapo Guzmán?"

We had a great time writing and sharing thoughts on serious topics. The majority of prisoners were Afro-Caribbean, but there were also Pakistani migrant youths and poor whites. I do have to say that in England—the home of the English language, a language I've mastered—I had a hard time understanding the prisoners, with their mix of Jamaican Patois and Cockney slang. I told them so. After three days of working together, I learned enough to follow along.

Lancaster State Prison is located in a desert within Los Angeles County, an hour's drive from my house in the San Fernando Valley. In over ten years of teaching there I've worked with a few "stars" of the system. One is Kenneth E. Hartman, doing life without possibility of parole (LWOP) for a murder he committed in 1980 as an alcohol-and-drug-crazed nine-teen-year-old. Kenneth later changed his life and helped create the first and only honor yard in the California prison system. His magazine writing and book, *Mother California: A Story of Redemption Behind Bars*, brought him awards and national attention. The governor commuted Kenneth's LWOP sentence, and in 2017, he was released after thirty-eight years. Then there is Stanley "Spoon" Jackson, another LWOP sentencee, already with over forty years behind bars, who has poetry books, musicals based on his writings, a memoir with my friend and fellow prison writing teacher, Judith Tannenbaum, and a prison production of *Waiting for Godot* to his credit. Or Tuan Doan, with his own novel about on a mother and son struggling to survive in war-torn Vietnam. And I can't forget Jimmy McMillan and Samual N. Brown, performance poets supreme, with hip-hop prowess, revolutionary ideas, and transformative visions coming at you from every conceivable angle.

All of these writers are gifted, disciplined, and, when I worked with them, as upstanding as any men I've ever known.

In the beginning, most of the men in my classes were African American. Because of prison politics, Chicanos at first were not attending my classes, even though they are the largest ethnic group in state institutions. But when word got out about what I taught—creative writing, but also creative thinking and living—and how I drew from indigenous cosmologies based in Mexico and the United States with a poet's heart, Chicanos began showing up. Many were already superb artists and wordsmiths. Soon there were waiting lists for those who wanted to take part.

One Chicano from A Yard, a former gang member who had done twenty-eight years, secured parole after letters were written on his behalf, including one from me. He had spent eight months in my class. He was published in the book I coedited with Lucinda Thomas, *Honor Comes Hard: Writings from the California Prison System's Honor Yard*, published by Tia Chucha Press. Out of prison now for several years, this *vato* has helped other formerly incarcerated and gang youth find their way in organizations like the Catalyst Foundation, Homeboy Industries, and Youth Mentoring Connection.

Of course, I've also had whites, Asians, and Native Americans in my classes. They all worked hard and produced exceptional work. No matter the issues and themes we explored, everyone respected one another regardless of cultural, political, and religious differences. I've had progressives and conservatives. I've had Catholics, evangelical Christians, Muslims, Native American spiritual practitioners, Buddhists, and atheists. All were welcome, all ideas were allowed.

There was one incarcerated man who wrote poetry in couplets and interesting turns of phrase. However, he became adamant about his right-wing ideology after Trump won the presidency. I was impressed at how nobody attacked him in class. I knew the majority in the class had political differences with him, but the protocol in the yard took over. People could say what they pleased, without being shouted down or berated. This didn't mean the dude went unchallenged—the guys were articulate in expressing their disagreements without animus.

One day, this prisoner read a piece that started out praising Trump early on in his presidency and saying the American people should give him a chance. But then he opened up about his own life: growing up dirt poor, his parents on drugs, offered only bad schooling and few opportunities, he felt blocked in, unwanted, unhelped.

When he was done I casually said, "Listen, if you just drop all that Trump stuff and get to your story—the challenges of poverty and closed doors, the barriers you confronted—then you got us. Now we can relate. It's the commonality of our experiences, regardless of race, that reaches us, not the beliefs or politics we can't agree on and therefore can't unite with."

The others in the class chimed in.

"That's right, ése, when you opened up about your family and everything taken away from you," one homie responded, "we were all there with you."

The dude thought about this. An epiphany seemed to cross his mind. Sure, our differences are real. But there are still things we share, experiences we can connect with—love, loss, joy. And through deep thought and knowledge, we can pinpoint a common cause to what ails all of us.

We may disagree on what's behind the rain. But if we don't want to get wet, we're all going to need umbrellas. On that we can agree. This understanding—about what's objective and undeniable—becomes the basis for common interests, common aims, common actions.

I've also realized how many people not behind bars—out in the world, working, raising families—are caught in their own "prisons": poverty, addiction, rage, a diminished sense of being, race and gender power trips. I've realized how men and women behind razor wire and in cages can be free with intelligence and imagination. I try to help give them those keys to freedom regardless of what holds them. Prisons are compressed and intense microcosms of the world, but they can also be powerful schools on how to live, how to become more human. And we still need actual keys to open up actual prisons, to find cures and changes outside of industrial incarceration.

In February 2010, I was in Chihuahua for a week, during a time when it was the most violent state in Mexico. It was bad in 1999, when I first visited the Rarámuri tribe of Chihuahua's

Copper Canyon. But things had become outrageous by my return.

In December 2006, then–Mexican president Felipe Calderón, with assistance from the George W. Bush administration, declared war on the country's drug cartels. Deaths attributed to this war have reached horrific proportions. Ciudad Juárez—in the border region where I was born—at the time had the world's highest murder rate: 330 murders per 100,000 people. In 2010, Ciudad Juárez had 3,100 murders in a city of 1.5 million people. Street massacres that year included 17 slaughtered in one party, 14 in another location, and 13 in still another.

After fourteen years of "war" against the cartels, some two hundred thousand people in Mexico have been killed—many cut up, burned, beheaded, bombed. Another thirty thousand have disappeared. This is more than the deaths in the Afghanistan and Iraq wars combined during the same period. While drugs inundated the United States to meet the demands of the world's largest drug market, US-manufactured guns went south. There is only one legal firearms dealer in Mexico; there are 6,700 licensed gun dealers in the United States along the Mexican border. Despite the anticartel war, Mexican cartels in that time period grew to be the most powerful criminal enterprises in the world, with greater inroads into the United States than ever before.

How do you go to war against something and make it bigger and stronger? In fact, the whole war on drugs, starting with President Nixon in the early 1970s, has cost more than $1 trillion in total (around $50 billion a year). This war has put tens of thousands of people behind bars and killed thousands more in Latin America and in US inner cities, only to see drugs become deadlier and more widespread than ever before.

It's a failure we keep feeding.

I spoke at the Autonomous University of Chihuahua to students studying native peoples. They explained that cartels use Native peoples as runners, and villages have been destroyed for the cultivation of drug crops. I spoke to mothers of some of the hundreds of girls and women killed since 1993—estimates have reached a thousand—in Ciudad Juárez's highly publicized "feminicide." They told me the kidnappings and murders have continued, although they've been pushed out of the headlines because of the drug war.

I traveled in and around Ciudad Juárez in a bulletproof SUV and stayed in a hotel where I was told not to go out at night. I spoke in the worst slums I'd ever been in (and I've been in some doozies): homes made of weathered wood planks held up with chicken wire, cardboard and plastic as walls and roofs. Sections of communities were named for the Mexican states people had migrated from—Veracruz, Guerrero, Oaxaca, and others. I visited libraries, schools, and community centers, and even performed poetry with local poets at the US consul's home, which was inside a gated community guarded by armed men and surrounded by a razor wire fence.

I entered Ciudad Juárez's juvenile hall and spoke to the youth, with TV cameras, radio mics, and print journalists on hand. I recall one young man, who had worked with a cartel before his arrest, responding to a reporter's question about why he did what he did. "Because I will never find a job, and if I do it will barely feed me or my family. That will be my lot till I'm an old man," he said. "But in the cartel, I can have the fanciest cars, the best clothes, eat at the swankiest restaurants, and be with all kinds of women. This will last, maybe, two years. Then I'll be killed, and most likely lose my arms, legs, and head. But for two years, man, for two years, I will have lived."

In Ciudad Juárez, I saw dead bodies on the street, surrounded by armed Mexican federal troops (by then, they had taken over the police department). In my talks, I related information about the urban peace work I did in Chicago, Los Angeles, around the United States, and in Central America. People were skeptical at first, but I presented an effective community-based gang intervention model. I had helped to create this model over a two-year period with around forty gang-intervention experts, truce leaders, and peace advocates.

In 2008, the Los Angeles City Council adopted this model. While the city did little to bring it to life, they did create twelve Gang Reduction and Youth Development (GRYD) zones in areas that had 400 percent higher rates of gang-related crime than other parts of the city. Their plan included "Summer Night Lights," which kept parks in thirty-two locations open late with sports, music, film, and more. Programs like this lowered gang violence in a city once considered the gang capital of America. Other intervention and peace efforts that were not sanctioned played major roles as well.

The response to this model in Ciudad Juárez was positive. Through a friend in the US Consulate's office, we got the document explaining our model translated into Spanish. A community group even started a book lending library called Mama Juana's with donated books, emulating the work of Tia Chucha's Bookstore.

Early in the trip, I entered a CERESO (Centro de Readaptación Social, a "Center for Social Readaptation") in Chihuahua City. However, before I was allowed to go in I had to convince the warden I was qualified. The US Consulate presented me as someone with years of experience in US prisons. The warden didn't think this was good enough. Then I mentioned I had worked with the *maras* of Central America. This convinced him I was worthy, although he emphasized that the prisoners I was going to address were survivors of a massacre of twenty inmates in a riot the year before in a Ciudad Juárez prison.

Since the beginning of Calderón's "war," there has been a rise in prison riots throughout Mexico. Many prisons were run by cartels or street gangs; guards guarded the periphery and never entered inside a prison yard. That same prison in Ciudad Juárez had another riot in 2011 that left seventeen dead. Later twenty-eight prisoners were killed in a riot in an Acapulco prison. In 2016, close to fifty people died in a prison battle between the notorious Zetas drug cartel and their rivals in the city of Monterey. Prison breaks also hit extreme levels, with 153 convicts having escaped a prison in Nuevo Laredo.

In the 2009 prison riot in Ciudad Juárez, a gang tied to one cartel battled with another gang linked to another cartel. Both gangs began in Texas prisons and, after their members were deported, combined with cartels to bloodier results. This craziness comes from historical trauma, including the infinitely destructive Spanish conquest; extreme poverty; the highly exploitative working conditions of multinational corporations; Mexican government corruption and neglect; US government impositions and manipulations; and, more recently, the mass deportations of US-based gangs and criminals to Mexico. All violence has roots. All violence, ultimately, makes sense no matter how senseless it may appear.

In the Chihuahua prison, I walked into a cellblock that held the group who had received the brunt of the attack from the year before. We had about two hundred guys in a dark room. At first all was well, as I talked about my books and the work I did turning around gang members and other troubled youth.

Then the warden showed up. All of a sudden, the prisoners' demeanor shifted. It turned out the warden had never set foot inside the prison walls. Now the men fixed their gazes on him, they stood up, and in bitter tones they complained about the terrible conditions they faced—no work, no training, no basic amenities. A gut feeling overwhelmed me, something I've learned to trust in these situations—the prisoners were going to kidnap the warden, and probably me as well. If this happened, we'd very likely be killed. The two guards with the warden were no match for the men. We were fucked.

So I did the only thing I could do. I began reciting a poem of mine in Spanish:

Pedazo a pedazo
te desgarran,
pelandote capas de tu ser,
mintiendo sobre quién eres,
hablando por tus sueños.
En el escualor de sus ojos
eres un criminal—vistiéndote en una chaqueta de mentiras—
hecha de acero a la medida,
eres su retrato perfecto.
¡Quítatela! Haz tu propio manto.
Desafía a los interrogadores.
Observa bien la muerte en su mirada.
Dí que no te rendirás.
Dí que no les creerás cuando te nombren de nuevo.
Dí que no aceptarás sus reglas, sus colores, sus morales depravados.
Aquí tienes un camino.
Aquí puedes cantar la victoria.
Aquí no eres una raza conquistada,
la víctima perpetua,
un rostro sombrío en la tormenta.
Manos y mente están esculpiendo un santuario.
Usa estas armas contra ellos.
Usa tus talentos dados
—no son de piedra.

I walked back and forth across the front of the room with increasing fervor as I recited more poems. At some point the warden left. The men turned slowly toward me, to my onslaught of words in cadence—words to make them think and feel. The cascade of language swam across oceans of neglect, death, and history. I didn't know if this would work. But it was the only weapon I had, my only defense, my only battle arms—poetry and more poetry. By the end, the men were listening to me again. Soon they relaxed. Everything calmed down. That's how quickly things can turn in prisons.

When I finished, the prisoners and I walked out into the prison yard. A photographer who had gone into the cellblock with me took photos. The rest of us chatted and laughed, as if we were at a park, taking in the sun, enjoying each other's company. Poetry and profound ideas still hung in the air, on this special day, a sacred day, a day without violence.

Men's Tears

"We should try to be parents of our future rather than the offspring of our past."
—MIGUEL DE UNAMUNO

As a tyke I disliked playing outside, running around, kicking balls back and forth, or scrambling in dirt and grass—unlike my older brother José, who used to rumble with neighborhood boys in dirt-clod fights. Armed only with plywood or trashcan covers, the boys, divided into teams, would throw dirt clods—often rocks covered in dirt—at each other. José had a scar from one childhood encounter when a projectile struck him square in the forehead. There was blood everywhere.

I preferred playing with toy trucks and army men, being in my head, making up dialogue and adventures. I was awkward, clumsy, behind the eight ball.

Once, at eight years old, when I was visiting my nieces in El Monte (they were only two and three years younger than me), José coaxed me into a homemade go-kart with a lawn-mower engine, painstakingly put together by an Argentine kid mechanical genius who lived next door to my nieces. I didn't want to get in the damned thing, but José's taunting got the better of me. I pressed my foot on some kind of accelerator. The go-kart took off. I soon found myself barreling toward a six-foot-high wood-stake fence. I didn't know what to do—turn, brake, or jump off. I just closed my eyes and crashed into the fence, wood splinters and engine parts flying up in the air along with me. I survived— maybe I was going ten miles per hour or so. But the go-kart was done, the Argentine kid in tears. I hardly lived that down.

Then, at nine, I was stretched out on the front porch playing with plastic toys and wooden cars when my next-door neighbor, a girl about my age, asked if I wanted to play dolls. I didn't think twice about this. I'd played dolls with my younger sisters from time to time. So then there I was on *her* porch, my Ken to her Barbie. As things would have it, a couple of local toughs happened to walk by—bullies. They snickered and kept on walking.

I caught hell in school. Students called me everything from "sissy" to "faggot" (and, in Spanish, even more unbearable terms). I didn't even know what "faggot" meant. I only knew I was being targeted for being "like a girl." Was that such a terrible thing?

One day, the two bullies saw me and started talking smack about José, who at the time was a school athlete and running star. I turned around and defended him—despite his abuse in the past, he was still my brother. That's all the excuse the bullies needed. One punch and I was on the ground. Somebody yelled, "Stay down!" I was disgraced, demeaned. I didn't get up, and the bullies laughed. Others joined in. One shook his head.

I told myself I'd never let anyone do this to me ever again.

Unfortunately, that punch fractured a section of my jaw, which I never took care of. I had a bruise over that part of my face for a long time. A growth developed in the bone. In time I exhibited a jutting mandible that brought more degradations. I was a skinny kid with a big chin. Kids made fun of me. I was the brunt of jokes. A girl called me "monkey."

Two years later I joined a gang. Not only did this give me status and a fighting chance, but also the homies embraced my most damaged feature. My gang moniker became "Chin." This was how I identified from then on. Even when my parents, who never had money, offered to pay to get my jaw fixed, I refused. This is something I regret now, more than fifty years later, as I only have three places where my teeth meet, a decades-long problem of not chewing well.

Once in a gang I was no longer bully fodder. I fought all the time. I took on all takers. I shot and stabbed people. I sat in jails and juvenile hall for mostly violent acts. I turned "crazy," a stone-cold purveyor of *la vida loca*—tattooed, needles in veins, feeling up chola girls in the shadows, with a façade of toughness to keep everyone away. The message: don't get close. I turned against parents, teachers, police, rival gang members, and even José, who once tried to reason with me. I was gone—into the street's steely snare.

Never again would anyone humiliate me.

I've come a long way in the decades since then. I've learned to overcome the limiting don't-fuck-with-me persona I fostered in my adolescence. The persona made me stop crying, stop feeling, hurt others before they hurt me—it made me the kind of man my society, my culture, my neighborhood demanded I be. We were all prisoners of patriarchy, which damaged women and children but also our masculinity, our humanity.

Unfortunately, these kinds of men tend to replicate themselves for newer generations, molding their sons—and daughters—to accept unequal relations and abuse. In time these men can be blocked by good reasoning, societal pressures, systematized responses, even laws. But to hold and sustain such changes requires a profound change at the level of society's base—the whole patriarchy has to be upturned.

Nevertheless, for years I've been working on breaking those

molds inside me. Today I freely exhibit sensitive, creative, and feminine qualities. I cry when I need to. I laugh much more. I can also show anger, but it is mostly contained within the boundaries of dignity and integrality; I try not to "lose it." This is not easy—especially since my sobriety forces me to regularly address the pressing pain beneath all the fury, instead of drowning it in drugs or alcohol.

I've acted out the tough-guy role most of my life. Now the feminine is unleashed in my writing, learning interests, community activism, and many other pursuits. Mind you, I also have strong masculine energy in attention to details, getting things organized, in moving projects. I protect my community, my family, and myself. I can stand up to most dangers. Together these energies, if properly activated, can make for a visionary *and* productive person.

What about being "tough"? It's better to be solid and aimed true. This also requires appropriate flexibility: as the saying goes, only trees with sturdy, profound roots withstand the strongest winds.

Being sturdy but flexible is even more important when one claims the mantle of healer and revolutionary. I'm now free to be the poet and imaginative person my inner drives always demanded of me. Far too many males remain constrained by their father's blows, mother's yells, peers' reprimands, social mores.

"Man up!" is the cry. But this is not only about *aguante*—the will to withstand whatever comes at you. We need to expand what our idea of "man" is and what withstanding consists of, to include the powers, emotional and otherwise, that anyone can retrieve.

Of course, one should have backbone, to endure the pressures and fires of life. This goes for men and women alike. These fires either forge you or melt you. When the latter happens it can lead to distortion, even to the grotesque, at the level of soul.

When the former occurs it can temper the steel of your character, to help focus your vision and action.

As a maintenance mechanic I used acetylene/oxygen cutting torches, among other tools. Imagine acetylene gas as masculine and oxygen as feminine: in proper ratio to each other, you get the most precise cutting flame. On the job, the right mix was when the emission coming out of the torch had a blue plume at its core. When there was too much or little acetylene in relation to oxygen, you either just blackened the metal you were trying to cut, or you melted it. The blue plume at the center meant you could make good, clean cuts.

Feminine and masculine energies are in nature, in our psyches, and in how we stand in the world. But we must remember: the feminine is constant, the masculine variable. Men need to adequately access both for a full emotional life—to show strength and stamina but also feel hurt, confusion, and doubt, and embrace whatever ordeals may come. Ordeals are what make a life.

It's especially important to have men's tears. I'm not talking about men who "cry" about so-called unfair situations, who complain (and "mansplain"), exhibiting an infantile outlook toward serious things. The tears I'm talking about are different from the tears of a child. These mature tears allow one to be present with healthy and authentic feelings. Unfortunately, rage is one emotion that frequently emanates from fractured and emotionally strapped men. Outrage and rage create explosive and dangerous situations at home, at work, and in public spaces.. Anger, on the other hand, is natural and necessary. Anger has eyes. Anger has source and direction, putting resolution within one's grasp. Rage, on the other hand, is blind.

With art, song, poetry, music, clear writing, anger can be effectively expressed. This is also true in personal arguments; one is generally in a good space of anger if they are able to maintain language, including biting wit and focused ideas. Anger loses its grip over us when fully addressed. As Emily Dickinson wrote: "Anger as soon as fed is dead— 'Tis starving makes it fat."

Arnulfo Timoteo Garcia was serving a twenty-five-to-life sentence in San Quentin Prison when I met him, more than ten years ago. He was editor of the *San Quentin News* and a leader in Guiding Rage Into Power (GRIP). From East San Jose, drug addiction had brought him to crime and prison. Close friends called him Pachuco, for the cool way he carried himself.

I once read poetry on San Quentin's maximum-security yard (at the time, overcrowding was so bad that all rooms were used for prisoner housing). With me were a saxophone player, a conga drummer, and the stories and words of Michael Meade, as well as the renowned American Buddhist Jack Kornfield, founder of Spirit Rock Meditation Center nearby. Arnulfo was our friend inside who helped host us.

I took part in another talk at the San Quentin chapel. A few years later I spoke during a public event with about three hundred outside visitors for a GRIP graduation. Arnulfo stood there in cap and gown, surrounded by other graduating prisoners. Everyone respected Arnulfo—*Sureño* and *Norteño* Mexicans, black and white, correctional officers and prisoners. He broke through walls with genuine heart and mind.

After serving sixteen years during his last stretch, Arnulfo was approved for early release—many people gave him glowing recommendations. We talked on the phone about the work we were going to do together—for urban peace, for justice, for personal and social transformations in our poor, diminished, and traumatized communities. I was always encouraged whenever we talked. He was one person who could make mountains move against any obstruction.

After Arnulfo's release, I got to see him as a free man during the fortieth anniversary of Barrios Unidos in Santa Cruz, California, on September 9, 2017. Daniel "Nane" Alejandrez, founder and director of Barrios Unidos, who has brought me to juvenile lockups and Soledad prison over the years, also knew and worked with Arnulfo. Barrios Unidos acknowledged Arnulfo and other men who had served many years in prison—including one who did close to forty years—and were now in community as leaders, mentors, fathers, grandfathers.

Arnulfo strolled about with a huge smile all night. He introduced me to his family. I brought my son Ramiro to meet this hero of mine. I also introduced Arnulfo to my friend and fellow peace warrior, Alex Sanchez, once a leader in the Normandy Locos set of Mara Salvatrucha and now founder and director of Homies Unidos, a peace and gang-interventionist organization working with Central American youth. Alex and I were once members of *Sureño* gangs. I told Alex that Arnulfo was from a *Norteño* neighborhood, and without hesitation, Arnulfo grabbed us both and gave us a loving hug. I was so moved by this gesture—for all the death, suffering, and destruction the wars between *Sureños* and *Norteños* have caused over six decades. And there we were, so-called enemies, in a powerful embrace.

It was a moment I will never forget.

Two months after Arnulfo became free in the world, he was in a car with his sister Yolanda Herrera, on the way to meet with community leaders, when a vehicle smashed into them from behind, forcing the car into the path of a semi-truck.

Arnulfo and Yolanda were killed instantly.

I've cried many man tears in the past decade or so.

My best friend in Los Angeles, Tony Hernandez, a Chicanoized Guatemalan cholo known as Crow, first contacted me from prison after reading *Always Running*. We became close after his release, when I learned he'd endured twenty years of drug abuse and seventeen years in juvenile lockups and prison, and had been shot. He was my biggest fan and always sat in the front row at my readings. Tony had been suicidal as long as I could remember. He lasted around a decade after being freed. I, and others, stopped him from dying many times. He had extreme intelligence; he loved books and spiritual matters (he was a practicing Buddhist). He became part of the Mosaic men's conferences in Mendocino, California. I paid to get Tony to Peru with Trini and me along with two other members of our sweat lodge circle. The Quechua recognized the Mayan in him and loved his likeable personality.

Tony seemed happy the last two weeks of his life. He built an interior wall for Tia Chucha's and helped us move from one space to another. He came by the house to share food and thoughts. Even though Tony and his longtime girlfriend had broken up, and he was in between jobs, he acted like he was okay. One day Tony asked me when I was leaving town again. He had asked this many times before. On this occasion I was leaving for Boston within days; I answered without thinking much about it. The night I arrived in Boston, I received a phone call: Tony had called a mutual friend to say he was ending it all with pills and beer in an undisclosed location. On the phone he said something like, "Tell Louie I love him and that I'm at peace."

Two weeks later a security guard making his rounds found Tony's body inside a pickup truck, parked in the wide lot of a warehouse complex.

A few years later, I received news that James Lilly, another one of my biggest supporters, from the Chicago area, was gone. The call came from our friend Izumi Tanaka, a photographer and filmmaker, who created a 2007 documentary on James's life called "Pushin' Forward: The James Lilly Story." James was a Mexican kid from the Little Village barrio, a former Latin King known as "Shyster," who had been paralyzed since being shot at fifteen. James eventually found his way, got married, had children, and even became a world-class wheelchair racer, one year winning the grueling Sadler's Ultra Challenge 267-mile run from Fairbanks to Anchorage, Alaska. James also attended more than a few of my talks, and I went to see him speak to kids as well. In his early forties, despondent and drinking, James killed himself in the garage of his home.

I felt guilty about these deaths. I felt I should have done more—the same way I felt about the two dozen homies and friends I lost in my youth. I carried this guilt, even when others explained to me I hadn't done anything wrong and probably couldn't have done anything to stop them. I understand. Just the same, I've ruminated over and over about how I could have been more sharply responsive to these brothers.

One of the heartbreaking losses of the past few years was Greg Kimura, a Japanese American poet who I'd known for close to twenty years from the Mosaic gatherings. He called himself the "Bad Poet" and he'd get up to read "bad" poems, but they were always insightful, with humor and depth:

> *Write bad poetry—make it rhyme.*
> *Invent weird rhythm that slips way, way, way out of time.*
> *Use trees, leaves and sieves as cheap metaphors.*
> *Steal 2nd-hand images like girlfriend-slammed doors.*
>
> *Be abstract, obscure, completely obtuse.*
> *Use ludicrous words like hypotenuse.*
> *And nasty words like shoot, heck, and dang.*
> *And wiener and spit and boom shangalang.*

Make darkness fall, make dawn arise.
Make the girl at the counter have cornflower eyes.
And don't worry about rhythm, 'cause this isn't rap.
Snoop Dogg don't write this kind of crap.

Make your pain sharp as needles.
Make your mother play kazoo.
(And use historical references
like Napoleon's Waterloo.)

Don't get hung up on rhyme.
Most call what I write poetry crime.
Just slip your hands in the deepest black muck
Slide your straw in and take a big suck
And most of all . . . write bad poetry.

Greg passed away in 2017 from a brain-stem tumor. But he smiled and held on to loved ones and friends, till the end. One story I've heard about Greg's influence was of a seventy-year-old woman who owned a home on South Pender Island, British Columbia. An American, she visited there often over thirty years. One day her thirty-six-year-old daughter saw a bottle floating near the island. She retrieved it and brought it to her mother. In the bottle, still dry, was a copy of Greg's poem "Cargo." The woman took "Cargo" to her friends, who all loved it. She then searched on the Internet for information about Greg and found out he had passed a few months before. Deeply saddened, she felt the synchronicity of coming across that poem when she did. It was an otherworldly gift from Greg to her and her family and friends—one, she said, she'd cherish.

All these men were decent and honorable, as were many others who've died who I can't name here. They were my friends despite whatever dogged them from their pasts, whatever personal demons they carried or whatever fate claimed them. I should point out that many more men and women I've helped or interacted with over the years who were tangled up with gangs, prisons, or suicide roads, or in recovery, are doing well. Most are enjoying stable lives. Nonetheless, these men are missed. Now they are ancestors—I call on them in times of need, being among the legislators of the dead whom I appeal to.

Here's Rumi:

> *On the day I die, when I'm being carried*
> *toward the grave, don't weep. Don't say,*
> *he's gone, he's gone. Death has nothing*
> *to do with going away. The sun sets and*
> *the moon sets, but they're not gone.*
> *Death is a coming together. The tomb*
> *looks like a prison, but it's really*
> *release into union. The human seed goes*
> *down in the ground like a bucket into*
> *the well where Joseph is. It grows and*
> *comes up full of some unimagined beauty.*
> *Your mouth closes here and immediately*
> *opens with a shout of joy over there.*

Men should cry more, connect more, feel more—and men and women should outcry more against men's abuse, power, control, addictions, and rage.

Cry and outcry.

At the same time, tears aren't always about deaths or other losses. There are also tears of joy; of comprehension; of the realization of wise outcomes, even when least expected; of reaching plateaus in life, without safety net or equipment, but moving forward anyway; of seeing how mentors, elders, friends, strong teachings, a great love, family, have lit the murky trails.

We've also cried too much—trillions of tears, so much pain, so much damage—and seen things remain the same. We've yelled and screamed, oh so often, with great intensity, railing and railing against injustices small and large, and still we feel invalidated and unheard. At some point the screams and cries, and the unfathomable numbness that can overtake us, are not enough. It's good that we can have an array of feelings, but in one's life, as in the life of a people, these have to turn into positive and formidable options. We all need a relationship with options—the more the better. These will help transform the hurt and rage beyond our fists, our bodies, our throats, and our silences into what's generative and healing and loving.

Collective hungers and angers should become artfully extracted into a culture of paying attention and acting accordingly, acknowledging the worth of every pain, every joy, all the tears, all the screams.

Dancing the Race and Identity Mambo

"Truth is beautiful ... but so are lies."
—RALPH WALDO EMERSON

Recently, my wife, Trini, and I decided to explore our ancestral DNA. We are living in pioneering times in this field. While
far from perfectly accurate, current DNA tests through online
sites provide percentage matches based on samples provided by
others. I'm aware they can be problematic: An African American friend of ours did a DNA test that claimed her ancestry was
from Eastern Europe!

These tests may all be scams. Yet if they land in the genetic
ballpark, they do yield interesting results. Trini and I undertook
this exploration not to confirm any "purity" or favored cultural
relationship but to get a glimpse of where we may have come
from (at least in the past thousand years).

To provide a context, Trini and I both identify as Native,
regardless of DNA: Trini to the Wixáritari/Mexica tribes of
Mexico and me to the Rarámuri/Mexica. The Diné roadman,
Anthony Lee, and his wife Delores, of Lukachukai, Arizona,
recognized this after we took part in prayer meetings and other
rituals on their land. In 1998, they spiritually adopted Trini. She's
been calling them "Mom" and "Dad" ever since. Trini takes this
seriously—these adoptions are not for show or status. (Her own

parents, now passed on, disowned her when she left home at twenty-one to finish college.)

Over twenty years ago we began to travel as much as possible to the Diné reservation for ceremony and family time. During one of those ceremonies, Anthony gave me a name in Diné: *Naayee' Neezghanii. This means "Monster Slayer," or "someone who has overcome many obstacles."*

Trini and I are also working class—that social class that must sell its physical, creative, or mental labor to survive. We were both born in the United States; Trini in Martinez, California, as part of the farmworking migrant stream with her family of eleven siblings. We identify as Xicanx, in deference to our Mexican migrant parents. This situates us, providing a framework to distinguish what we are, not to separate ourselves or be classified into notions of superiority or inferiority.

In addition, we know we are culturally and "racially" diverse—like most Mexicans. A recent genome study in Mexico showed it is one of the most diverse lands on earth. This study proved Mexicans are more native than anything else—at least 60 percent, taking into account all the people, including 26 million tribal peoples, more than any country in the hemisphere. And its people are more African than is often recognized: in one state, Guerrero, the people were 22 percent of African descent. And many Mexican people's DNA has strong traces of Europeans (Spanish and others), Middle Easterners, Asians, and more.

Before I reveal our DNA results, I'd like to delve into this whole "race" thing. In dissecting race as a concept, every which way possible, the hope is perhaps it will die of a thousand cuts. Race has been with us far too long—since Europeans first arrived in the Americas, and later with the birth of the USA—as a destructive and nagging presence. This county's foundations are intertwined with it. In the United States there's always some kind of "race" card being played.

We are forever dancing the race-and-identity mambo.

Holdovers of this habit include when so-called scientists measured people's craniums to determine inferiority, or when one's social status depended on how much white, black, yellow, or brown "blood" one had (blood, of course, has no such colors). Even the concept of "Caucasian" is racist—originally the term meant the people from the purported "Garden of Eden," where human beings were said to have originated. In the 1700s, "scientists" and "philosophers" (Christoph Meiners, Johann Friedrich Blumenbach, Carl Linnaeus, et al.) falsely determined this was in the area of the Caucasus Mountains, home to the "superior" race of all races!

Another terrible example of this never-ending dance was when Spanish elites instituted the *casta* race system, whereby pure "white blood" Spaniards born in Spain were the most valued, and other categories were undervalued in layers: *criollos* (Spaniards born in the Americas), *castizos* (Europeans with some Native), *mestizos* (Natives mixed with Europeans), *cholos* (Natives with *mestizos*), *mulattoes* (Africans with Europeans), *pardos* (Europeans, Africans, and Natives), *indios* (Natives), *negros* (Africans) . . . and so on, including categories involving Chinese and other peoples.

All of this is made up.

"Whiteness" is in fact a big fat lie, concocted to favorably distinguish Europeans from dark-skinned people. This is the ultimate "identity politics." Nothing in biology, in objective reality, exists to assign any superiority to skin color. Having different skin colors is what humans consist of—that's just a feature of who we are, one that tells nothing about our characters or innate geniuses. The actual idea of race is unsound at all levels—except as a political and historical monstrosity, except as a power relation.

In addition, "white" as a racial category has moved around over the years. At various times in the United States, Arabs and Latinos were given "white" status. In Texas, Mexicans were considered "white." If you look at my birth certificate from El Paso, my parents were labeled "white" although my mother was mostly Native and my father's background includes Native, Spanish, and African ancestors.

"White" can be a label of convenience. Hitler, for example, declared Germany's Japanese allies and Turkish SS troops "honorary Aryans." When my family first moved to California, we lived mostly with blacks—restrictive covenants in housing limited where we could reside because in California we weren't "white" anymore. In fact, many Mexicans lived with blacks in South Los Angeles, Pacoima, Compton, Inglewood, and similar areas because of these covenants and because of real-estate interests redlining housing tracts to exclude them.

Human beings have established social systems, racial categories, social classes, and more out of lies and absurdities for millennia. Such deceptions are made to appear real although they are patently untrue. To make "believers," the powers that be have used books, movies, pseudoscientists, schools, military might, laws, and even religious institutions (which can claim "God's" authority) to get the rest of us to go along.

Many "official" bodies, often touted as trustworthy, have fantasized alternative realities and spent public and private resources to propagate them. Think of what Hitler and his sick stalwarts did, and now see how other so-called leaders of government, corporations, and even educational institutions have done the same—some more benign, some worse and more sophisticated than Hitler.

Societies have consistently pulled the wool over our eyes—

and I'm not just talking about run-of-the-mill con men, street-corner hustlers, or swindlers. I'm talking about kings, emperors, presidents, senators, generals, TV personalities, teachers, preachers, and even parents, those with power and voice to speak over the rest of us. While many people will be "had," the majority of us must smarten up.

Of course, beliefs, faiths, and spiritual practices, which have come down to us from since humans first walked the planet, are natural, part of our rich imaginative life. That's the tension. Stories and mythology are ingrained in our metaphor-/symbol-making brains. This is who we are. But those with power and wealth often mutate such mythic-poetic impulses to deceive and confuse the majority for their benefit.

One way they do this is to render stories, parables, and myths as "objective." Literalizing distorts the understanding that stories, myths, and similar creations are the "lies" which hold our truths. These myths teach, inspire, and motivate by tapping into the image-receiving part of our makeup. If we literalize the stories, they can trap and paralyze us in falsehoods.

Think again about "race" and "blood." When Europeans arrived in 1492 to the so-called New World, rape, pillage, murder, and racial categorization came along with them. All were justified by rendering *less* human the people they encountered. Even popes got in on this act.

Prior to this invasion, Polynesians, Japanese, Chinese, Norsemen, and even Africans were said to have made their way to "Turtle Island," as many US tribes called the vast hemisphere. These early arrivals interacted and traded. Some stayed and had families. But they didn't conquer or destroy, and none of them seemed to care about "pure blood."

Another muddled idea is the misnamed "Western civilization." While this term may not be solely about race, I've heard it used to mean "white" without explicitly saying so. For example,

Iowa Republican congressman Steve King remarked during the 2016 Republican Convention: "Go back through history . . . where are these contributions made by these other categories of people that you are talking about? Where did any other sub-group of people contribute more to civilization?" MSNBC's Chris Hayes then asked, "Than white people?" King responded, "Western civilization itself, rooted in Western Europe, Eastern Europe, and the United States, and every place where the foot-print of Christianity settled the world."

Unfortunately, Hayes didn't challenge King's assertions. He called them "self-refuting." But they *do* need to be challenged. For as wrong as King may be, there are whole infrastructures in our country that keep these ideas palpitating. Even presidents of the United States espouse them.

Let's be clear: what we consider Western culture was *not* born in a vacuum or developed solely by Europeans. So let me take on Congressman King's challenge.

For thousands of years, Europeans absorbed song, science, medicine, religions, music, foods, and so much more from others—be they from Africa, China, India, the Middle East, Asia, the Pacific Islands, or the so-called New World—including appropriating them for advantage and exploitation. This was largely possible because Europe is the "world island," contiguous to Asia and the Mideast and a stone's throw from Africa.

Marco Polo's travels to China, Jewish diasporas, Muslim rule in southern Spain and Italy, invasion of and theft from the so-called Americas, the opening and subjugations of India and Africa, all provided material as well as cultural wealth in the arts, literature, and sciences attributed to the European Renais-sance of the fourteenth to seventeenth centuries. Just correlate the times and events.

Prior to that, from Africa and the Middle East arose three of the world's most important religions: Christianity, Islam, and

Judaism. The first "cradles of civilization"—where the conditions converged to establish forms of writing, agriculture, architecture, governance, and more—were along the Niger River (West Africa), the Nile Valley (Egypt), the Tigris and Euphrates Rivers (Mesopotamia), the Indus Valley (India), the Yellow River (China), and in Mexico and Central America ("Meso-America"), and the Andes.

None were in Europe.

From South and East Asia came Buddhism, paper, fireworks, oranges, porcelain, fishing reels, suspension bridges, tea, and medicine, among others. From Native peoples of the "Americas," the world obtained maize, tomatoes, avocados, potatoes, rubber, hummingbirds, democratic forms, irrigation, herbal healing, astrology, calendars, and more. From Africa came musical instruments (guitars, drums, harps), mathematics, astronomy, engineering, medicine, and navigation, to name a few.

Even Homer the "Greek," considered the "Father of Western Literature," whose stories were said to be conveyed orally for a thousand years beginning around the eighth century BC, may have had African origins. If this is not the case, such stories were similarly told for thousands of years in Africa through *griots*—poets and storytellers. It does not serve truth telling to insist on separation from the Mother Continent, even if later there were other directions and embellishments in such stories in the Mediterranean region or elsewhere.

European nations and companies looted the "New World" and Africa of gold, silver, diamonds, and other minerals, which made many of those countries the first world colonial powers and sparked capitalist development. There are still churches in Spain, as well as the Basilica in the Vatican, with inlaid gold and gold statues made from this theft. There are museums throughout Europe with the largest collections of preconquest artifacts anywhere, the majority hidden in basements and vaults.

And in the United States, we can't forget the legacy of African enslavement, along with land stolen from Native Americans through genocide and mineral- and oil-rich territory conquered from Mexico (60 percent of Mexico's natural resources were taken in the US invasion between 1846 and 1848, including oil reserves that would have made Mexico the world's largest producer). Over time, these resources propelled the United States to the height of wealth and militarization among nations.

Free land, free labor, free access to minerals and oil—a country where bodies, land, and what the land provides have been *owned*—are enough to make any country "great."

US culture is a product of the whole world, not just "Anglos." If you've ever flown a kite, barbecued, surfed, participated in martial arts, bounced a rubber ball, chewed gum, eaten a chocolate bar, used a compass, witnessed a fireworks display, visited a library, smoked a cigarette, enjoyed a chili pepper, or drunk tea or coffee, then you've done things originally from Africa, South and East Asia, the Middle East, the Pacific Islands, and Native America.

When I was growing up, schools and other institutions hounded Blacks, Mexicans, Asians, Natives, and others to "assimilate" into so-called Anglo culture. This meant submitting to world cultures rendered through the prism, often violent, of US history, laws, and politics, including a race- and class-based lens.

Of course, most peoples of the world have adapted to, assimilated into, or appropriated from other peoples—yet few to the extent that Europeans or US people of European ancestry have done. Does this mean that Europeans didn't contribute anything significant? Of course not—Europeans and European-descended peoples in the United States have deep, formidable imprints in technology, industry, science, governance, literature, and art.

You can't take anything away from anyone.

But that's the point—include everyone! To address Congressman King, or anyone else who claims otherwise, European contributions (or misrepresentations of such) cannot be an argument for superiority. Only conquests and power dynamics sustain such thinking. All of us, from whatever culture or so-called race, have added to the world's layered development, both good and bad, both marvelous and disastrous.

And what about "white nationalism"? Well, show me this "white" nation. Europe today is made up of people of all skin colors, religions, outlooks, and more, as is the United States. And I get particularly perturbed when people talk about the "white" working class. There is only one working class—and it's made up of whites, blacks, Latinx, Asians, Native Americans, men, women, all sexual/gender orientations, migrants, and immigrants. Any talk about a "white" working class serves only to put a wedge between lighter-skinned workers and the rest of us. That way our interests as a class are divided along superficial lines.

Again, you wouldn't know this if you went by official history books or textbooks, or watched most TV shows and movies, in which the roots, trunks, and branches of human history and development, its multiplicity and flowering, are erased or diminished. The lies are pushed on us by elaborate systems calculated to dictate our lives. They are maintained by force. Hence we in the United States have the world's greatest military power and domestic police state. Schools, media, and the entertainment industry sustain these fabrications. Now and then, we are allowed entry as well as a good time. We're bribed into believing this is all inviolable.

It's a massive con. Billions of dollars are spent to keep us under its spell. Still this brainwashing is less and less available or effective, forcing direct power to be deployed against people deemed disloyal or a threat. This is not about any "deep state."

It's about the *whole* state—what you see and what you don't. Our loyalty, our passivity, our turning a blind eye, being victimized and loving it, is the end game. Like many Americans—and people around the world—I'm done with being manipulated, used, with being the chump who keeps buying into a system that keeps slapping me in the face.

A big antidote to the lies, this poison, is truth, which isn't hard to uncover despite the vast expanse of doctored videos, alternative facts, and cherry-picking of reality or books in social media, TV, radio, and in the halls of government. Do the work! The antidote is here, among us, with those who do not overvalue or undervalue humanity based on class, race, or sexual preference. The antidote is with those of us who have our dignities intact—and don't try to take away anyone else's dignity.

Now for those DNA results. Interestingly, Trini and I have similar breakdowns. The biggest chunk of our DNA is Native American, close to half of our total DNA. This is native from the whole hemisphere; the tests at the time didn't break down "Native America" more precisely. Still, they revealed almost 50 percent of our DNA is tied to all indigenous people of so-called North, Central, and South America.

The tests indicated we also have African DNA—mine was linked to North Africa, Benin-Togo, and Mali. Trini's was from Benin-Togo, North Africa, and Southeastern Bantu. This makes sense due to the African presence in Mexico. We also have remnants from the Middle East and Asia. With all this, we each have close to 60 percent DNA from people of color. As for European strands, we are as diverse as you can imagine: Trini has traces of Eastern European, Scandinavian, Western European, British, and European Jewish DNA. She is about 25 percent from the Iberian Peninsula (Spain/Portugal), but she is also 9 percent from Italy/Greece. I have traces of Western European, Scandinavian, Eastern European, European Jewish, and Irish DNA, and 8 percent from Italy/Greece.

What threw me off is this—13 percent of my DNA is from the Iberian Peninsula. I thought it would be more. But the kicker is that I am 13 percent from Great Britain (England/Scotland/Wales). I have no idea where this strand of my history came from, but there you have it.

According to these samples, Trini and I have the whole world in our DNA. What a fascinating mix of humanity. Even if the tests are not totally accurate, we are still citizens of the planet, unbounded in many ways. With these DNA results you can see the tremendous impact of worldwide migration patterns, trade, wars, conquests, and other interactions, good and appalling, across history. We embody many stories, a rich tapestry of colors, dialects, skins, and beliefs.

Nevertheless, our biggest DNA bloc from these tests is Native American. It shows we have ties to this land as deep as anyone's. As we stay attendant to the indigenous, we can also appreciate the rest of humanity that came together at one time or another so both of us could be born, marry, have children, and help shape the world.

However, when Trini and I related our DNA results to our Diné elder Anthony, he remarked that this was charming, entertaining perhaps. But he also admonished us—we are not fractured persons, with this drop of blood and that drop of blood. We are not mixed up (mestizos). The Diné recognize each other through an extensive clan system, which includes clans for Hopis, Pimas, Zunis, and Mexicans (*Naakai dine'é*), among others, due to intermarriage. None of this means we are less or more.

"Remember," our elder said, "you are whole and complete as you are."

The Story of Our Day

"Without the right to dream and the waters that it gives to
drink, the other rights would die of thirst."
—EDUARDO GALEANO

A few years ago I made a presentation at a weeklong writers
conference in Idyllwild, California, where I also taught poetry
to aspiring writers. In my talk I broke down the main tenets of
indigenous thought. Afterward, a kindly older man walked up
to me. He said he was a retired marine, interested in writing,
and enjoyed my talk. However, he wanted me to accept that the
best thing the United States ever did was the US Constitution.
Although he didn't say this, I could extrapolate that he meant
what "white people" in the United States ever did.

I waited a beat before responding, as calm and centered as
I could be, commensurate with his manner. I told him the US
Constitution was an undeniably important document—the law
of the land. And yet its major ideas and philosophies, including
about democracy and representative government, were already
in existence before any European set foot on these shores.

The man's face grew puzzled. He then thanked me and
stepped away.

There's been a case made that the so-called Founding
Fathers borrowed from Native Americans' existing gov-

erning principles, in particular from the Iroquois Confederacy (People of the Longhouse). Perhaps, but if they did, they didn't incorporate the more equalitarian aspects. For example, the Five Nations of the Iroquois (which later added another tribe to become six) were matrilineal; clan mothers chose the leading representatives. Most historians conclude, however, that US governing theorems were modeled from the patriarchal mindset of the Greeks, the English, and other Europeans. And, as in most of Europe of those times, inequality was built into these ruling systems.

For Native Americans, the US Constitution was for all intents and purposes a limited warranty. It spelled out "rights" that actually curtailed the freedoms indigenous people already enjoyed, even if unwritten. The first peoples here didn't need a piece of paper to recognize, nurture, and live by essential agreements. For them, nature—everything from the smallest organisms to the vast cosmos—was their constitution.

When ratified in 1788, the US Constitution also circumscribed voting rights. Most states insisted on enfranchising only white men with property. There were also compromises with slaveholders, like counting enslaved Blacks as three-fifths of a person to give Southern states more congressional representation, even though enslaved people weren't considered human and couldn't vote.

After some 240 years, several battles, mobilizations, rulings, legislative amendments, marches, riots, and war, the country extended constitutional rights to women, who gained the right to vote in 1920; Native Americans, who weren't considered "citizens" until 1924; Blacks, Mexicans, other communities of color, and the disabled, who received civil and voting rights in 1964 and 1965; and LGBTQ persons, who finally saw a Supreme Court ruling in favor of same-sex marriage in 2015.

I'll quote none other than Thurgood Marshall, the first

African American Supreme Court justice, from his 1987 speech during the Constitution's bicentennial:

I do not believe that the meaning of the Constitution was forever "fixed" at the Philadelphia Convention. Nor do I find the wisdom, foresight, and sense of justice exhibited by the Framers particularly profound. To the contrary, the government they devised was defective from the start, requiring several amendments, a civil war, and momentous social transformation to attain the system of constitutional government, and its respect for the individual freedoms and human rights, we hold as fundamental today. When contemporary Americans cite "The Constitution," they invoke a concept that is vastly different from what the Framers barely began to construct two centuries ago.

Nobody gave anybody anything—every extension of rights had to be fought for, at the cost of thousands of lives. Whether *de jure* or *de facto*, by law or by practice, discrimination and disenfranchisement had to be named and justice actively pressed for.

Obviously there's immense value in the US Constitution. But, again, we should stop whitewashing history. It's also a negligible argument that these rights have to be "earned," something early European settlers never had to do in relation to their Native and Black brethren.

For all its importance, the US Constitution can't seem to stop the rise of autocratic presidents and narrow-minded governing bodies. Using the Constitution, the most deceptive of politicians or agency officials skillfully attempt to pull a fast one on most of us. The current political and economic order has now become the order of *chaos*, wherein the natural laws that can help everyone are discarded for capricious laws that cause more damage. Chaos and instability are characteristic of the prevailing administration, Congress, and even the Supreme Court.

Checks and balances? These are largely nonoperational.

Even with all the mountains of tax revenues flowing into government coffers, we still don't have a right to the best possible healthcare or free and quality education for everyone. Laws should guarantee freedom from insecurity for all people, not just to those who can afford it. How does an advanced and developed country continue to tout itself as the "best" in the world when our reality is lacking a moral, humane foundation?

The crux of our social, political, and economic crises is linked to our coerced allegiance to empire. The US military budget is bigger than the combined military budgets of China, Russia, the United Kingdom, Japan, France, Saudi Arabia, India, Germany, Italy, and Brazil—$682 billion to $652 billion. The United States is going the way of all empires, into an implosion amidst a growing stridency. Empires are said to last, at the most, around a thousand years. Hitler's Third Reich was supposed to last as long but didn't go beyond a dozen years thanks to successful opposition (although at a loss of sixty million lives). The United States can also fall into this ensnarement—or we can curtail our decline by rising up to meet this country's great promise and hope. Estimates now claim that US-involved or -orchestrated wars, invasions, coups, interventions, and proxy wars may have led to twenty to thirty million deaths since the end of World War II.

The real battle is for the soul of America.

In 2014, I managed a seemingly foolish move, against all odds and with literally no chance of success: I ran for governor in the most populous, costliest, and most economically divided state in the country—California.

I decided to undertake this campaign when every political party and movement in the United States was deeply in crisis—when society was rent with irreparable economic and political ruptures, when outmoded industrial capitalist models/concepts were dying, while new forms of organization, relationships, and governance struggled to be born.

I couldn't have done this without the support of my family—who backed me knowing I'd put in inordinate time and effort, which pretty much truncated my ability to hustle work, thus affecting whether I could keep the household going.

I couldn't have done this without the well wishes of the community centered around Tia Chucha's Centro Cultural and Bookstore. Although the Centro didn't endorse me or use its funds or offices for the campaign (it's a tax-exempt corporation), I ran knowing the space might suffer—since our inception I had helped do outreach and fund-raising with our board and other volunteers (although Trini and her staff were the ones who actually made everything happen).

I had already run for US vice president in 2012 on the ticket of the Justice Party USA, with Salt Lake City's former mayor Rocky Anderson as our presidential nominee. I traveled to a few cities and received coverage in important progressive media outlets such as Pacifica Radio's *Democracy Now!* Rocky represented a strong voice against corruption in politics and against the "duopoly"—one party with two faces, masquerading as choice. The Justice Party was able to make the ballots of fifteen states, and obtain write-in status in fifteen additional states, to garner around forty thousand votes in the national election.

So, just before I turned sixty, I offered this potent sacrifice—in the sense of a sacred act—for a new campaign. At the time I felt that after more than forty years of revolutionary teaching, organizing, and writing, I had to take all this to heightened levels of influence and impact. This wasn't about being a better governor; I offered myself as a *different kind* of governor.

I understood the electoral platform had for the most part lost major relevance in the country. It was a feeble and largely inapt space, but one I didn't think should be turned over to corporate interests without a fight. I'm also aware of Republican efforts to purge voters from the rolls and set up obstacles to voting in mostly poor communities of color. And evidence has been found of Russian trolls and others influencing campaigns. All these efforts, in my view, were to push aside revolutionary visions and voices, new ways of thinking and articulating.

What underlies this imbalance is deeper, wider, and cannot be corrected within the current capitalist system—a just, peaceful, and green world is simply irreconcilable with a profit-motivated paradigm. Still, we must stretch the system beyond its limits. We must try. We must actively pursue this within the reality that democracy has been largely bought and sold.

Reforms should push forward revolution, and revolution should complete all reforms.

The Democratic and Republican Parties have become drenched with big money. With the 2010 Supreme Court ruling in *Citizens United v. Federal Election Commission*, upholding the "right" of corporations to make political expenditures, obscene amounts of capital entered even the smallest, and seemingly most inconsequential, elections. Elections are another industry—the 2016 national election was the most expensive yet, costing around $2 billion, while mass media made a killing on ads and commercials.

Campaign-finance reform arose to limit the way corporations, banks, and lobbyists swayed and controlled the American vote. The more control big money had in voting, the more removed the process had become from the majority of the American electorate, especially its working class, now being driven to abject poverty and homelessness. The pervading economy in the country's most deprived areas has been dominated by Walmart, which became the largest employer in many of the formerly industrial and agricultural powerhouse states of the Midwest and the South. Nobody employs more people in the private sector throughout the world than Walmart. The world's largest government employer is the US Department of Defense.

That's not to say there aren't decent and principled Democrats, or even Republicans. But despite courageous politicians who still understand the selfless nature of public service, the institutional powers are not really interested in true representation.

At the time of my campaign, California was the sixth largest economy in the world, the most developed and wealthiest state, yet with a 24 percent poverty rate—higher than the poverty rates of Mississippi and Georgia. The state had a multibillion-dollar prison industry that garnered more tax dollars than colleges and universities. It had opened the door to "fracking" (hydraulic fracturing) that poisoned land and water tables with hundreds of cancer-causing chemicals and tons of gallons of waste water blasted to extract oil from shale while energy companies extracted vast profits. California also had the most migrants to the country, yet was seeing increased deportations and the building of privately owned detention centers alongside the fact that many of its major businesses, particularly in agriculture, were dependent on low-paid migrant labor. Here was a state with the largest companies in the defense industry plying for a war economy while core urban areas became battlegrounds for street and drug gangs—with law enforcement agencies as the largest "gangs" to curtail them. We were also the fiftieth worst state when it came to arts funding—and forty-eighth worst in education funding.

I love California, its people, the land, but not everything it had become. The state's economic and political difficulties could not be solved by superficial economic or political policies, or by passing laws or initiatives that kept the system intact. Something bigger was missing—an *imagination* for a new California.

I asked my friend of four decades, Anthony Prince, a revolutionary lawyer and strategist, to be my campaign manager. He was actually my campaign manager in 1976–77 when I ran for a Los Angeles school board seat (I was twenty-two then, living in Watts). For the new campaign, we had a number of volunteers meet regularly at the guesthouse in my backyard. We embarked on a journey of no return—with little in the way of funds, around $30,000 at the end, against an array of fifteen candidates whose frontrunner had up to $20 million at his disposal. We ran against a relatively popular sitting governor, Jerry Brown, on his fourth run for the office since he first became governor in 1975.

In tiny, cramped rented cars, Tony and I (as well as activists of the northeast San Fernando Valley) drove up and down the state a dozen times—to the Central Valley, the Sacramento Delta area, the Bay Area, the Inland Empire, and other parts of Southern California, including the border area, coastal cities, and deserts. We faced a new primary structure where only the top two candidates (regardless of party) would make the ballot in the general election. Of course, I wouldn't take corporate funds. We had to go grass roots all the way.

Since party-nominated candidates were no longer allowed to run, I had to get the endorsements of important parties and organizations. Even though I ran as an "independent," I received the invaluable endorsements of the Green Party of California, the Justice Party USA, the Mexican American Political Association, and El Hormiguero (the Anthill), an activist collective, among other individuals and organizations. Even the "Dean" of Chicano Studies, Professor Rudy Acuña, who rarely gave such support, endorsed me.

Although I had a hard time attracting major media attention, since my money didn't talk loud enough for them, I did pull off coverage from the Huffington Post, Fox News Latino, the *Los Angeles Times*, Truthout, MintPress News, Radio Bilingue in the Central Valley, KPFA and KPFK radio stations in the Bay Area and Los Angeles, and others.

I also ran for governor of California at a time when the country felt divided between the "good" guys and "bad" guys. The "good" guys—the so-called functional and "normal" people—supposedly have rights over everyone else, though they are often behind some of the most maddening and destructive ideas, acts, and laws in this country.

As far as the NRA is concerned, they *are* the "good" guys. The Second Amendment allows for a carefully regulated militia against tyranny, our right to "bear arms." But many Americans are more worried about the tyranny of the NRA, which pays government officials millions of dollars—including $30 million to Trump's campaign—for the "freedom" to own as many guns, including assault rifles, as possible, which is *not* part of the Second Amendment.

These "good" people include the Confederate flag–waving Americans who've idealized a past that never existed while going to war against a present and future they've distorted to fit their ideological prism. They include major sections of law enforcement, our "protectors," who are *trained* to kill at any sign of danger, yet "danger" isn't hard to find, judging by the many instances where unarmed people—mostly Black, but also poor brown and white persons—have been killed by police. They include Americans applauding "smart" bombs and sending our young men and women to wars that destroy other people's homes, families, and cities to protect our so-called interests— oil, commerce, and power. They include law-abiding members of our urban, suburban, and rural communities, also struggling, also struck hard by economic disasters, yet secluded and often kept ignorant, since learning is for the "educated elite."

As one racist Mississippi sheriff told a reporter following the lynching of two Black teens in 1942, hung from a bridge before a throng of spectators, resulting in no arrests: "We're all for law and order here. But, of course, we got some *good* folks who get kind of wild." (Emphasis mine.)

The "bad" guys are the rest of us who may not fall into the above categories: so-called inner-city folk, migrants of color, the mentally ill, organized labor, trans folks, the so-called "entitled" poor accepting welfare and other social services . . . I can go on and on. Just having different ideas can place you in this excluded group. Just not loving America the way "good" people say you should can get you shouted down with "Leave it!"

I'm tired of living under the oppression of hypocritical, superinflated, self-proclaimed "good" people and their politics of rage.

We're told to believe capitalism has mystical powers. But there's nothing magical or sacred in the so-called marketplace. In fact, capitalism is not the same as the marketplace, which has to do with exchange and has been around since before capitalism and will be there afterward. Capitalism is primarily a unique relationship based on the large-scale theft of surplus value—the amount workers are *not* paid for their labor, generating incalculable profits. A small (and decreasing) number of the rich and powerful end up controlling land, minerals, air, water, oil, factories, etc. as private property. To hide this relationship, capitalism upholds illusions that are meant to appear formidable and irrevocable; mortgages, the stock market, borders, money, credit, and wage systems are all deceptions cloaked in life-and-death garb. These concepts are made up—as are white supremacy, the rule of wealth, and often the explanations for when and why we go to war. We should remember that to remove illusions about any situation is to remove situations that require illusions.

With this understanding, in my campaign I also called for the eradication of poverty. I knew this required bold imaginings and systemic changes. An economy so dramatically transformed by automation and globalization demands an equally transformative vision for jobs, housing, healthcare, and education. The yardstick for this new economy should be simple: decent working and living conditions for all. I had to make a case that the social inequities we currently face are not natural disasters. They are human-made and can be changed by human minds, hands, hearts, and technology.

For example, after a spate of bad subprime mortgages and other made-up financial instruments sparked the Great Recession of 2008, millions of people lost their homes, their livelihoods, and in some cases their lives. This didn't happen overnight. The groundwork had been laid decades before. This included the 1978 legal challenges to state usury laws, allowing banks to promote credit cards to consumers; the 1982 congressional deregulation of the savings and loan industry; and the repeal in 1999 of most of the Glass-Steagall Act, a Depression-era law that separated commercial and investment banking.

While millions of households suffered, a few wealthy investors benefited, including real estate magnate Donald Trump. The Great Recession became a monumental transfer of wealth from the so-called middle class to the richest percentile. Government should have been there to help those most affected. Instead the US Treasury Department in late 2008 paid out $700 billion to bail out banks (the full commitment since then has been calculated at close to $17 trillion!). Big banks got bigger—they got rewarded—despite their complicity.

What keeps the majority of American people from rebelling, from upturning all the tables on the corporations and their congressional and media henchmen? As before, we are mostly in a fog of delusions that keeps us bailing water in the face of a sinking economic *Titanic*.

In the California governor's campaign I proposed four pillars of a thriving and healthy society. Martin Luther King Jr. proposed such pillars just before his death in 1968. He knew any new societal structure had to have strong supports to hold everything on solid footing.

Here, in summation, are the pillars: 1) A clean and green environment for all; 2) Social justice, including an end to mass incarceration, police killings, and discriminatory practices; 3) The end of poverty, since whenever any people are poor, no matter what society claims, we are all poor in moral as well as material ways; and 4) Peace in the world and peace at home.

All of this should be undergirded by a truly transparent and publicly financed corporate-free democratic process.

As King also stated, these pillars cannot be built under capitalism. They are contrary to a system of production and politics based on the bottom line. Further, all the pillars are linked. They are inseparable as we go forward—we cannot have environmental health or social justice as long as there is poverty, and there can be no peace without environmental health and social justice . . . Every pillar is intertwined with the need for fundamental systemic change.

I felt we needed to connect the dots and not be divided by "my" issue over "yours." I had to illuminate a vision to fully address the earthquakes shaking up the state—not just the natural ones but the economic, social, and political quakes millions had already suffered through, and the many more to come.

There were many highlights of the campaign, like when I spoke at a candidates' event at Los Angeles Pierce College in the San Fernando Valley—the school where my father worked as a laboratory custodian for fifteen years. Or when I visited a couple of times with family and supporters in the vacant lot where a Sonoma County sheriff's deputy in Santa Rosa killed thirteen-year-old Andy Lopez when the deputy mistook Andy's toy gun for the real thing. Similarly, I went to the memorial site where San Francisco police officers killed an unarmed security guard, Alex Nieto, in Bernal Heights. And I marched with hundreds against the police killing in LA's Venice community of an unarmed homeless man as gentrification threatened to throw more people into the streets.

I marched through housing projects and streets in Watts with students, parents, and teachers for resources to help our schools. I received a great response from African American and Chicano Studies classes at Fresno Community College. I spoke out against the removal of poor and elderly people from their homes in the rapidly gentrifying city of San Francisco, including to a rousing gathering in old Manilatown. I addressed the largest homeless enclave between San Francisco and Los Angeles in Salinas, whose leaders are now part of one of the most important organizing efforts by the displaced, a National Union of the Homeless. In addition, I marched with four thousand people protesting the police murders of five unarmed Mexican and Central American farmworkers within two years in that city.

Corazon Del Pueblo, *Brooklyn & Boyle* magazine, and others from Boyle Heights organized an astonishing event called The Poetry Locomotive. Supporters jumped on the Metro in East Los Angeles, reading poetry on the trains while making various stops at stores, taco shops, and community centers. From there community members and myself read poetry and spoke on the issues. The locomotive ended at LA's Union Station, where a growing number of people amassed to hear poetry, speeches, and words from key supporters as well as Trini and myself.

In the end, with hardly any funds but tons of energy, ideas, and volunteers, we beat out all candidates but five with close to seventy thousand votes. We were first amongst third-party and independent candidates. In San Francisco, I finished second after Brown. And I won precincts along the Mexican border. Of course, I didn't make it out of the primary elections, but we changed the larger conversation on the issues.

We made a case that a new economic and political reality was possible.

Every age has its story—the mythology of the day, if you will—which corresponds to real, objective forces. I'm trying to get at the unfolding revolutionary process from another angle, one that maintains the content of our times, based on what's actually happening, and examines how this intersects with story, the imagination, the subjective.

I'm trying to see spirit and science properly joined.

An important aspect of any story that dares to indicate where we are as a culture and a people, as well as where we're going, is how imagination intersects with the revolutionary potential in society. This includes the thorough integration of the arts into daily life, and not just as a nice thing to do, for pleasure, or to pass the time (although the arts provide all these things). As society moves toward a more creative/inventive stage in history—based on digital modes of production and other advances—we can enliven this statement: to become a complete human being is to become a complete artist.

The path out of chaos is not order. It's creativity. We need a society that applies its wealth and production to this aim—that every human being should be healthy in body, mind, and spirit, able to access their innate genius to make their creative and indelible mark in this world.

We are living in perilous times. Most everything is up in the air—economies, politics, families, work, structures, and ideologies. At the same time, antiquated philosophies are being given new life (white supremacy, for one). The past is tearing apart the present. The present appears to be on skates, racing downhill with no brakes. And the future looms with a challenge—can we make the right societal choices, move away from contrived scarcity into plenitude, strengthening crucial relationships that renew life and our humanity?

Can we have healthy and strong people on a healthy and strong planet?

Even before my run for California governor, it became evident to me that the global "left," whatever had resulted from revolutionary thought and organization during the last two centuries, was floundering. If everything is in crisis, so are organizations that claim the mantle of revolution. This makes sense and is quite necessary. Much of the left acts as if it is immune from a process affecting all institutions and organizations.

Revolutionary organizations must change or die—change the form to save the content. The content, however, is shifting as the economic base of society shifts: robots in the workplace and computers at home. Revolutionaries and activists that are succeeding understand that motion isn't about how fast things are going but their direction—and how we can invigorate new ways of getting there. As the ancients have done in other times of crisis, at other social crossroads, they turn to creativity.

Art is the pathway.

The next stage of human development is integrality, the

unison of science, art, and morality. This dynamic development can only happen when society is no longer based on class rule or private property—the private ownership of the principal means of production, but also of Earth's minerals and energy. There are means and energy that are common to all of us—and they should remain as part of the commons to be safeguarded.

The resulting degree of wellness must guarantee everyone has their own authority, the clarity of their own minds and hearts, and is allowed to tap into their own unlimited capacities, while at the same time it must propel the collective to ensure everyone is taken care of materially, spiritually, and psychologically.

Again, all of this is unequivocally incompatible with global capitalism. Therefore the predicament we face is this: Can humanity continue to move forward while in the stranglehold of an economic and political system whose driving force is obtaining maximum profit regardless of its impact on people and planet?

The simple answer: no, we can't.

For the first time, humanity is faced with the need for evolutionary growth of our planet that is not just contingent on organic biological changes (following Darwin's law of natural selection), wherein external pressures force corresponding internal alterations so a species can persist or perish. Today aligned ideas, plans, technologies, and governance must be brought to bear, or we will fail to move to the next stage of our existence.

Consciousness *and* creativity are now vital to our future.

We are in a time of a true awakening: a time to know instead of to believe, to think instead of react, to imagine better instead of staying caught in a discordant class-based matrix. Certainly, the paradigm shift is a weighty proposition, full of risks, with seemingly insurmountable complications and no palpable guideposts. This is because we are embarking on what Joseph Campbell called a "pathless path." It's not a road less traveled but one we have to make ourselves: untrodden, its endpoint appearing as a question mark. Most people talk about this path as it relates to individuals. I apply the principle to societies as well. While this is untried territory, there are echoes of this journey from deep in our past.

It's time for revolutionary activists, thinkers, and artists to help draw out the multiplicity of powers within everybody, including the genius for social revolution. We need to teach each other and engender another generation of visionary *and* practical leaders to contend with and counter the unraveling social fabric. Our goal must be to unite the scattered movements whose shared aim is to honor humanity and the earth into a powerful moral force to realign the prevailing system of production, distribution, and rule. And as everything changes, we must maintain the rhythm of alignments as needed.

In this quest, we must not fall into the traps of the old left, which generally defined itself as against the political system, as anticapitalist, but was largely unable to envision a new reality—unless it was within the strictures of the industrial stage of development. This is quite a jig to dance, one that promises many slipups and stumbles. But stumble we must if we are to go forward into the spiral of advancement.

To reiterate, the once heroic and amazingly responsive left—socialists, communists, radical Christians, anarchists, antifascists, and all stripes in between—have been largely placated. At the same time, far too many revolutionaries are characterized by infighting, big egos, and self-sabotage, even beyond that caused by police agents and disrupters. Some of the bickering that prevails on social media is childish and debilitating, exhibiting the same contempt toward allies we disagree with as toward the foremost perpetrators of social inequities. When we treat the not-so-cool progressives as badly as we treat the social class enemies trying to cut our throats, most people can't tell the difference between them. The result is a deepening rift among masses of people, communities, and objective movements, rather than organic, lasting bonds.

Just the same, the recent rise of the alt-right has put some steam into activism, more animated now than in decades past. And there are people on the left who continue to forge those bonds between allies, who are moving roughly but steadily into the wealth of imagination and ideas we need for a new America.

How to proceed? What stories can possibly carry the vigor and appeal of what must be done?

First, the divisive racial story we have long told ourselves cannot hold as firmly as before. Neither can the "there are no classes" story or the concept of the trickle-down "generosity" of the capitalist class. The distractions are endless. Even if many of these narratives still gather momentum, those trains are, for the most part, coming to a halt.

This is not just about competing narratives—it's about clear lies versus clear truths.

Second, it's important to note that churches, unions, community organizations, nonprofits, trailer parks, and other similar spaces often *not* considered part of the revolutionary milieu also have the potential for stirring new ways of thinking, organizing and change. We have to go beyond preconceptions and consider the very real, although perhaps hard to fathom, prospect that revolutionaries may also come from among evangelicals and conservatives.

What's happening right now is the right is hell bent on blaming the left—and minorities, migrants, and movie stars—

and bending the truth to do so. And the left is keen on targeting the right, which at times can be a more precise aim. But the point is, right or left, we're all screwed.

Going after each other on this basis gets us nowhere. The economy doesn't care if you're Tea Party or Green Party or no party. It doesn't care if you are white, black, brown, red, or yellow, doesn't care what religion you abide by or if you abide by no religion, doesn't care if you like hamburgers, tacos, or jerk chicken. *It doesn't care.* As in a flood, if you get caught up in the torrent, those factors, which many people allot grave importance to, won't stop you from drowning.

For sure the most conscious among us will have to sway millions of religious people. And they can't be berated, knocked around, or scared into going along. All of them are gathering at the crossroads of change with the rest of us. Many are already reimagining their circumstances by returning to the revolutionary tenets within their own doctrines.

And yet there are already communities pissed off and moving—the undeterred women, youth, immigrants, LGBTQ communities, communities of color, the artists, the unemployed, students, and more who are in some ways the least invested in keeping capitalism going. They run the gamut from class conscious to variably socially conscious to downright apathetic. They number in the millions.

What stories and strategies can possibly pull together such a range of people in the United States? This requires reaching out beyond the obvious differences to the pressing concerns affecting most everyone—again, ending poverty, peace at home and abroad, environmental health, and social justice; the pillars that hold up sustainable and equitable societies.

Splintered responses to these concerns only hurt us.

Our stories can continue to cherish the long-held US ideals of freedom, fairness, and equity, not the ciphers and codes that have kept us divided. We must make sure our future is in accord with our best natures, of being wholly conscious, philosophically mature, global in content, local in form, and unable to be taken off track.

We are following a historical gradient. Doing so means we can't be afraid of mistakes. Fear of mistakes is tantamount to fear of growth. Yet grow we must. The point is to make mistakes in a principled way, toward more inclusive and widening nets, instead of mistakes in the direction of subterfuge, disguise, living in fear, essentially being "safe" at the expense of making history—what I call the politics of paranoia.

This isn't a call for provocative, heavy-handed, or reckless tactics—or to be naïve about the power of government to crack down on dissent and strategic activism. This is a call to be bold, to think big but also in steps that "aim little to miss little" (words from Rev. William Barber).

Our gauge should be the revolutionizing practice of the working class and poor—the more conscious and united they become, the better we will know our influence and strength. Any self-respecting revolutionary has no other measure. Either our ideas are grasped by a significant number of people who are prepared to carry out corresponding actions, or we have not done what we set out to do. There can be no more schizophrenic divisions between "leaders" and "followers," teachings and practice, "authoritative" people and so-called nonauthoritative people, theory and reality, a "mass" way and a "class-conscious" one.

Again, we need stories, which are also schools, but we also need other sense- and spirit-activating mediums. Stealth is the way to do battle under the radar, so to speak, without drawing unwanted attention, yet spreading ideas through the powers of the pen, the paintbrush, the drum, the dance . . . as well as the Internet, smart phones, apps, and podcasts. Subtlety is the art of refinement, the way to wield effective language, aesthetic qualities, and resonating designs. This is battle without doing battle.

And still the war is upon us.

Of course, we should prepare for actual battles. We can't doubt the ruling class will react as they always have—with fear, force, and deflection. They are doing so at this moment. The growing militarization of the police, whereby the brutality of wars in Iraq and Afghanistan is replicated at home, is their answer to increasing poverty and growing discontent. Their answer includes the gathering armies of white supremacists and right-wing extremists. People are being killed. The police juggernaut strikes hardest at the Achilles heel of US capitalism, the African American people, who are disproportionately targeted by police and mass incarceration, and who have historically had the most consistent response to oppression.

But the long-range target is the rest of us.

My campaign for governor was worth every mile traveled and dollar expended. It proved to be a milestone. The campaign provoked exhilarations and disappointments, but also critical lessons that could serve as a foundation for other campaigns. We won without winning. Right after the elections we began gatherings of the California Network for Revolutionary Change. A few people running for office in other parts of the state, and even a campaign in Chicago, told me the "Imagine a New California" campaign served as their model.

One thing I learned was that reaching people by way of stories means they plug into revolutionary politics and activities by connecting to their own stories, regardless of ideologies or beliefs. This approach is different than using ideology as the main way to plug people in, since the latter requires they only do so by accepting one "idea," one way, one connection—extremely limiting. Although ideology is important, it cannot solely determine our overall interests, strategies, and motion—real things in real time do.

Monotony expresses the concept of "one tone," which is tiresome and repetitive. We need to speak, write, and act in many tones, reaching through a range of sentiments, to move in many rhythms.

We must also master how to speak, write, teach, and organize, driven by the artful competence in each of us. Complex ideas must be expressed simply and clearly and resonate with emotional depth. We must use "aesthetic arrest" to get people to stop and think; we must be heartfelt to reach millions.

Art is the nexus of imagination and technique.

I learned on this governor's campaign that we don't have to be "amateurs"—as if all this is new. Humanity has been struggling for justice and equity since time immemorial, albeit at lower levels than we are now. But we also can't act like we know it all—there has to be room for innovation. New times call for new tactics.

Young people have this quality: they want to be part of something earth-shattering but shaped by their own authentic powers and imaginations. Elders can guide, teach, impart knowledge, hold the ground, but they can't lead everything. We must challenge the official stories as well as the scarcity thinking and living within the framework of the fear-driven precepts of the prevailing ruling class, its political parties, and its mass media. This is not an attempt to move toward "the middle," which politicians generally do, not fundamentally changing their positions but only their message so they can attract voters. Nor is the goal to be "populist," sacrificing long-range values for short-range acceptance.

Going back to the US Constitution, we may not be ready to face this, but after more than two centuries we should consider a new constitution, incorporating the most enlightened, encompassing, and equitable knowledge about matters of civil rights that has been accumulated from around the world, not just the United States. We need a document indicative of a time when we didn't need papers to convey what should be, by birthright, everybody's freedoms, while pointing to a time when government stops managing people and instead manages social structures for the enhancement, benefit, and health of all people and the living Earth.

To borrow from John Lennon: Imagine a world free of banks, corporations, high-end developers, wars, and poverty; imagine a world free of hunger, injustice, homelessness, and despair. Imagine a new Congress that honors ancestors and the living, made up of decent, dynamic men and women, representative of the country's vast expanse of skin tones, tongues, cultures, genders, and faiths. Envision what kind of world is arising, already pulsing through its people, including the poor, the deprived, already beating in their hearts, in their songs, in their best dreams for America and the world.

If all life is made up of stories, there is a story we are living out now. It has a three-act structure, with beginning, middle, and end, as well as setting, characters, conflicts, crisis, motive forces, more crisis, fatal flaws, resiliency, catharsis, and resolution. Like most stories in our culture, it has an intention—figuring out how to get us back home. Reaching back to Homer's *Odyssey*, getting home has been a recurrent theme in most of modern literature—home not just as a place but inside oneself, in our own hearts and at the heart of who we are as a people.

There's an ending to our story. Like all endings, it's also a beginning. Still we have a charge: To make the well-being of every child, adult, elder, family, and community the cornerstone of any new social compact, any new society, and the central quest of a new story. Any political party, news medium, organization, nonprofit, religion, or business must take this into account to be part of this great adventure.

It's time, finally, to come home.

Acknowledgments

Much love and respect to the amazing editor, teacher, organizer, and community healer Trini Tlazohteotl Rodriguez, now with thirty-five years as my partner/collaborator/best friend, including as my wife. And much love and respect to my children, Ramiro, Andrea, Ruben, and Luis; my grandchildren, Ricardo (Yei Iztcuintli), Anastasia, Amanda, Catalina, and Jack Carlos; and my great-grandchildren, Xavier, Jaydda, Andre, and Liliana.

Special thanks to Irish American mythologist and story teller Michael Meade for his longtime friendship and powerful teachings, and to the healing community of the Mosaic men's conferences in Mendocino, California (a'ho Duncan Allard, et al.)—I'm honored to have been a poetry teacher and mentor for these and other Mosaic conferences for over twenty-five years. Thanks also to Anthony and Delores Lee of Lukachukai, Diné Nation, and their family for their love and embrace of their daughter Trini and our family. Thanks to Mark Silverberg for editing and writing suggestions. And a huge *tlazhokamati*, thank you, to the amazing board, staff, and volunteers of Tia Chucha's Centro Cultural and Bookstore in the northeast San Fernando Valley, including the Mexica *kalpulli*s and *danza* circles, as well as Native American organizations and activists among the Chumash, Tataviam, Tongva, and other first peoples.

Credits

A version of "The End of Belonging" appeared as a column in the Huffington Post on November 15, 2011, and in blog posts for the Los Angeles Public Library website and on www.luisjrodriguez.com, as well as in the University of Oklahoma's *World Literature Today: Activism Issue* 93, no. 3 (September 2019). The poem *"Alabanza*: In Praise of Local 100" is from the book Alabanza: New and Selected Poems 1982–2002 by Martín Espada (New York: W. W. Norton & Company, 2004). Used with permission.

Most of "The Four Key Connections" appeared as a blog post based on a keynote speech I gave in 2014 at the 10th Annual J. Paul Taylor Social Justice Symposium at New Mexico State University, in Las Cruces, on "Justice for Native Americans: Historical Trauma, Contemporary Images, and Human Rights." It became the basis for a TEDx talk I gave in Venice, California, in October 2017. It also appeared as a blog post on the Los Angeles Public Library website, August 17, 2016. In this work, I drew from information and knowledge in the books *Nahui Mitl: The Journey of the Four Arrows* (Mexico City: Mexicayotl Productions, 1998 by Tlakaelel of the In Kontonal Center (Mexico City); *Cosmic Mayan Manual: Wizard's Oracle* by Tascara Patala (Los Angeles: The Mayan Center, 1998); a series of books by Mexican indigenous teacher Arturo Meza Gutiérrez from the

Kalpulli Toltekayotl, Mexico City; writings from and talks with Anthony Lee of Lukachukai, Arizona, on the Diné Nation; the writings of Dr. Roberto Cintli Rodriguez; and the teachings of: Cozkacuahtli Huitzilcenteotl of the Kalpulli Tloque Nahuaque in LA's San Fernando Valley; John Chee Smith of the Diné Nation; Macuiltochtli of Chicago; Julio Revolorio of Guatemala; Edilson Panduro (a Quechua traditional healer from the Amazon forest of Peru); Ed Young Man Afraid of His Horses of Pine Ridge, South Dakota; Tekpaltzin (Frank Blazquez) and his wife, Xochimeh (Lou), of Albuquerque, New Mexico; the Rarámuri of Cusárare, Copper Canyon, Chihuahua, Mexico; Zapoteco leaders in Juchitan, Oaxaca; Pipil elders in Izalco, San Salvador, El Salvador; and my friend, the poet and activist John Trudell.

A version of "Nemachtilli: The Spirit of Learning, the Spirit of Teaching" appeared in the National Council of Teachers of English's *English Journal* 94, no. 3 (January 2005).

Versions of "Constant State of Pregnancy" have appeared as speeches as well as blog posts over the years on www.luisjrodriguez.com.

Versions of "Poet Laureate? Poet Illiterate? What?" have appeared from 2014 to 2015 as blog posts on the Los Angeles Public Library website and on www.luisjrodriguez.com.

A section of "I Still Love H.E.R." appeared in *U.S. Latino Literatures and Cultures: Transnational Perspectives* (Fall 2000), a journal published by Universitätsverlag C. Winter in Heidelberg, Germany. The poem "Civilization" appeared in *My Nature Is Hunger: New and Selected Poems, 1989–2004* (Evanston, IL: Curbstone Books/Northwestern University Press, 2005).

A version of "'Low and Slow' in Tokyo" appeared in *Bella* magazine in September 2007, and in Santino Rivera, ed., *Lowriting: Shots, Rides & Stories from the Chicano Soul* (Broken Sword Publications, 2014). A passage was published in the online magazine *Pocho* ("Tokyo: Living La Vida Lowrider," February 12, 2014, http://www.pocho.com/tokyo-living-la-vida-lowrider-by-luis-rodriguez/) and in California's *Westways* magazine ("Lowrider Love: An L.A. Poet Reflects on One of SoCal's Gifts to the World," July/August 2018.

"Prickly Pear Cactus: Experiencing Los Angeles with Other Eyes" was originally written for *Wundor City Guide Los Angeles*, edited by Matthew Smith (London: Wunder Editions Ltd., 2018). Some of this material also appeared in the anthology *LAtitudes: An Angeleno's Atlas*, edited by Patricia Wakida (San Francisco: Heyday Books, 2015). This essay includes writings over the years from the *Progressive*, the *Nation*, the *Los Angeles Times*, and more. Parts of this essay also appeared in the introduction to *From Trouble to Triumph: True Stories of Redemption from Drugs, Gangs, and Prison*, by Alisha M. Rosas (San Fernando, CA: Tia Chucha Press, 2017) as well as the foreword to *Smile Now, Cry Later: Guns, Gangs and Tattoos—My Life in Black and Gray*, by Freddy Negrete and Steve Jones (New York: Seven Stories Press, 2016). The excerpt from "Love Poem to Los Angeles" is from *Borrowed Bones* (Evanston, IL: Curbstone Books/Northwestern University Press, 2016).

"Monsters of Our Own Making" draws from writings in the *New York Times*, *Los Angeles Times*, *Chicago Tribune*, *Christian Science Monitor*, *Guardian*, *San Bernardino Sun*, and *Huffington Post*, as well as blog posts on the Los Angeles Public Library website and at www.luisjrodriguez.com. The poem "Poverty of Access," by Jeffery Martin, was published in *The Coiled Serpent:*

Poets Arising from the Cultural Quakes and Shifts of Los Angeles, edited by Neelanjana Banerjee, Daniel A. Olivas, and Ruben J. Rodriguez (San Fernando, CA: Tia Chucha Press, 2016). Used with permission of the author. "Pedazo a pedazo" appeared in *The Nobody* (Pullman, WA: University of Washington, Spring 2003); *Crossroads Magazine* (Oakland, CA: December 1995/January 1996); *Trecero Festival Mundial de Poesia—Venezuela 2006* (Caracas, Venezuela: Fundacion Editorial, El Perro y La Rana, Spring 2007); and *Desperate Literature: The Unamuno Author Series Festival, A Bilingual Anthology* (Madrid: Desperate Literature, Spring 2019). Special thanks to the Alliance for California Traditional Arts for allowing me to teach the Lancaster State Prison classes I've cited here. Thanks also to the Trauma to Transformation program of Tia Chucha's Centro Cultural and its funders, the Art for Justice Fund and California Arts Council, for supporting our arts-based work in prisons, juvenile hall, parolee housing, and with families of the incarcerated.

Other versions of "Men's Tears" have appeared as blog posts on www.luisjrodriguez.com and the Los Angeles Public Library website. Greg Kimura's poem is from his self-published 2013 book *Cargo*. Rumi's poem is from *The Soul of Rumi: A New Collection of Ecstatic Poems*, trans. Coleman Barks (New York: HarperOne, 2001).

A version of "Dancing the Race and Identity Mambo" appeared in blog posts for the Los Angeles Public Library website.

A version of "The Story of Our Day" appeared in *'White' Washing American Education: The New Culture Wars in Ethnic Studies*, edited by Denise M. Sandoval, Anthony J. Ratcliff, Tracy Lachica Buenavista, and James R. Marin, vol. 1, *K–12* (Santa Barbara, CA: Praeger, 2016). A version was also presented as a paper in 2015 at the Second California Network for Revolutionary Change Conference at the XL Public House, Salinas, California. Parts were also taken from a blogpost at www.luisjrodriguez.com and a January 2017 episode of the podcast *The Hummingbird Cricket Hour*.

About the Author

From 2014 to 2016 LUIS J. RODRIGUEZ served as the official Poet Laureate of Los Angeles. He's the author of fifteen works of fiction, nonfiction, memoir, poetry, and children's literature. His most recent memoir, *It Calls You Back*, was a finalist for the National Book Critics Circle Award. He's been the recipient of many awards and fellowships, including the Lila Wallace-Reader's Digest Writers Award, Lannan Foundation Poetry Fellowship, Carl Sandburg Book Award, PEN Josephine Miles Literary Award, and more. A script consultant for the FX drama *Snowfall*, he founded Barking Rooster Entertainment, a production company for film, TV, web, and other content. He founded the well-respected Tia Chucha Press close to thirty years ago, which publishes mostly poetry collections, and is co-founder of Tia Chucha's Cultural Center & Bookstore in LA's San Fernando Valley. In addition to traveling extensively, he teaches every week at two maximum-security yards at Lancaster State Prison. www.luisjrodriguez.com.

About the Publisher

SEVEN STORIES PRESS is an independent book publisher based in New York City. We publish works of the imagination by such writers as Nelson Algren, Russell Banks, Octavia E. Butler, Ani DiFranco, Assia Djebar, Ariel Dorfman, Coco Fusco, Barry Gifford, Martha Long, Luis Negrón, Peter Plate, Hwang Sok-yong, Lee Stringer, and Kurt Vonnegut, to name a few, together with political titles by voices of conscience, including Subhankar Banerjee, the Boston Women's Health Collective, Noam Chomsky, Angela Y. Davis, Human Rights Watch, Derrick Jensen, Ralph Nader, Loretta Napoleoni, Gary Null, Greg Palast, Project Censored, Barbara Seaman, Alice Walker, Gary Webb, and Howard Zinn, among many others. Seven Stories Press believes publishers have a special responsibility to defend free speech and human rights, and to celebrate the gifts of the human imagination, wherever we can. In 2012 we launched Triangle Square books for young readers with strong social justice and narrative components, telling personal stories of courage and commitment. For additional information, visit www.sevenstories.com.